W9-CLU-991

ST. MARY'S COLLEGE OF MARYLAND
ST. MARY'S CITY, MARYLAND 20686

Navajo Tribal Demography, 1983–1986

Contemporary Issues in Health, Vol. 2
Garland Reference Library of Social Science, Vol. 846

NAVAJO TRIBAL DEMOGRAPHY, 1983–1986

A Comparative and Historical Perspective

Cheryl Howard

GARLAND PUBLISHING, INC. • NEW YORK & LONDON
1993

© 1993 Cheryl Howard
All rights reserved

Library of Congress Cataloging-in-Publication Data

Howard, Cheryl.
    Navajo tribal demography, 1983–1986 : a comparative and
historical perspective / Cheryl Howard.
        p. cm. — (Contemporary issues in health ; vol. 2)   (Garland
reference library of social science ; vol. 846)
    ISBN 0-8153-0888-4
    1. Navajo Indians—Population. 2. Navajo Indians—Statistics.
Vital. 3. Navajo Indians—History—20th century. I. Title.
II. Series. III. Series: Garland reference library of social
science ; v. 846.
E99.N3H78   1993
304.6'089'972—dc20   92-39357
                                                                      CIP

Printed on acid-free, 250-year-life paper
Manufactured in the United States of America

CONTENTS

SERIES PREFACE

The health conditions of American Indians remain a serious challenge to our society. In 1955 when the United States Public Health Service assumed responsibility for providing health care for American Indians, J. Nixon Hadley, statistician with the Division of Indian Health, stated:

> Measurement of health conditions among the Navajo is hampered by lack of complete data either on the base population involved or on death and illnesses. Even with this lack of specificity, however, it is obvious that mortality and morbidity rates for most of the major diseases are far in excess of the rates for the total United States population. (Adair, et al. 1988, p. 17)

Seventeen years later, E.A. Mares (1972) wrote "at the present time, the health status of the Indian population is about that of the rest of the United States twenty to twenty-five years ago. While the Indian birth rate is considerably higher than that of other Americans, life expectancy for the Indians is shorter compared to other Americans. The infant death rate is significantly higher for Indians than it is for other Americans. While the neonatal death rate of Indians is now about the same as the rest of the general population, the postneonatal death rate for Indians is still about three times higher than in the general population" (p. 17).

There have been some signs of improvement in the health of American Indians since 1955. Infant death rates and deaths from influenza, pneumonia, gastritis, and tuberculosis have all declined. Nonetheless, many of the health problems of American Indians continue to resemble those of Third World countries. It behooves epidemiologists, demographers, and social and behavioral scientists to assist health care professionals to better understand the unique culture of various American Indian tribes, their social organization, health values, health beliefs and health behavior, and the changing demographics of their societies, if we as a society are to help improve their health. Not all American Indians are alike and, therefore, respect and understanding for their differences is a first step toward working together to reduce mortality and morbidity.

Dr. Cheryl Howard's contribution to this series on Contemporary Issues in Health monitors how far we have progressed in reducing disease mortality among the Navajo between 1983–1986 and presents continuing and future challenges to controlling disease mortality among this growing ethnic group. Future challenges are illustrated by data from recently published studies which report that motor vehicle injuries are the second leading cause of death among American Indians; rates of adolescent suicide in the United States are highest among American Indians; Navajo adolescents have a high prevalence of obesity; hypertension is becoming more common among Navajo people; the prevalence of diabetes and its complications among Navajos appear to be increasing; and frequencies of colorectal and biliary tract cancer have been increasing. Much remains to be done. New, sustained collaborative efforts like the Many Farms Project of 1955–1960 are needed to bridge the gap between culture and health. Improving the health conditions of American Indians is a continuing challenge to modern public health and preventive medicine.

John G. Bruhn, Ph.D.

REFERENCES

Adair, John, Kurt W. Deuschle, and Clifford R. Barnett. *The People's Health: Medicine and Anthropology in a Navajo Community*, 2nd edition. Albuquerque: University of New Mexico Press, 1988.

Mares, E.A. *Selected Characteristics of New Mexico Culture*, Part 12, New Mexico Regional Medical Program, May 1, 1972.

INTRODUCTION

The United States is a post-industrial nation with the demographic profile of a post-industrial nation; but this belies the great diversity of fertility and mortality patterns found among different groups of people who inhabit this country. One such group is the American Indian.

Despite wide variation in cultural practices and historical conditions among tribes, patterns of fertility and mortality have long been different for American Indians compared to the U.S. population. In general, American Indian vital rates, life expectancy and median age of the population have resembled those of developing countries more than the U.S.

American Indians are an important segment of American society, both historically and today. Too little is known about the demography of this rapidly growing group. Furthermore, the Navajo are a matrifocal society, and the effects of this organizational structure on fertility and mortality are not well-documented, particularly in industrialized nations. The purpose of this investigation will be to analyze recent (1983–1986) vital statistics data on Navajo Indians to examine temporal trends, to compare the Navajo with all Indians and with other U.S. ethnic groups, as well as with total U.S. population data.

These data should sharpen our understanding of the dynamics of population and development in highly differentiated societies. Several theoretical perspectives will be evaluated against the findings reported here for "goodness of fit." A major focus of this research is to identify the value and shortcomings of the various theoretical perspectives with regard to the population under study.

The Navajo comprise approximately 17% of the total American Indian, Eskimo, and Alaska Native population residing in areas covered by the Indian Health Service. Further reference to all Indians in this report includes all three groups. Detailed information about data presented for all Indians is discussed in a later section.

The Navajo reservation lies in the arid, high desert plateau and mountains of northeastern Arizona, northwestern New Mexico, and a small portion of southern Utah (Figure 1); it is approximately the size of West Virginia (Spencer & Jennings, et al., 1977). The landscape is nothing short of spectacular: rugged mountains and mesas, wind- and river-carved canyons. The Navajo call their land *Dinetah* and themselves *Diné*, the People. In some respects, geography has been, and continues to be, a major determinant of Navajo destiny.

Let us first turn our attention to these people, who they are, where they come from, and how they have fared throughout history.

FIGURE 1
Map of Navajo Reservation

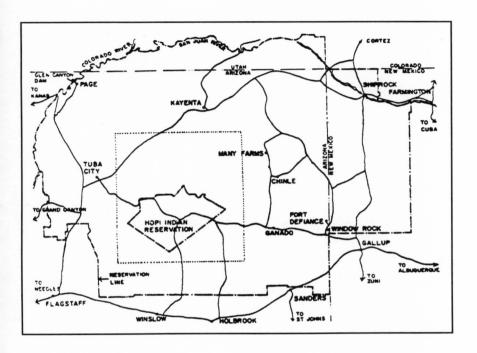

Source: Johnson, B.M., ed. *Papers on Navajo Culture and Life*. Tsaile, AZ: Navajo Community College Press, 1970.

NAVAJO TRIBAL DEMOGRAPHY, 1983–1986

Chapter 1

BACKGROUND

Early Population Size

There has been much speculation on the size of the Indian population of North America before European contact. The main purpose of speculation on early population size is to assess the damage of European contact upon the indigenous population, and to monitor the growth of tribes since. Methods of estimating this population have been of several types: ethnohistorical, relying on direct observations of individuals at the time of contact; archeological and physical anthropological data; ecological evidence; demographic and epidemiologic information; and information about the social structure (Thornton, 1987). Some scholars have used combinations of approaches. The range of estimates has varied from about one million (Kroeber, 1939; Mooney, 1928) to 9.8—12.25 million (Dobyns, 1966).

More recent analyses of precontact population size have been undertaken by Thornton (1987) and by Ubelaker (1988). Ubelaker used a synthesized tribe-by-tribe approach; his estimates for North America (including Alaska, Canada, and northern Mexico) range from a possible 1.2 million to 2.6 million, with 1.9 million as a best guess. An obvious problem with this approach is that entire tribes vanished before a record of their existence was noted. Thornton and Marsh-Thornton (1981) estimated precontact population in the conterminous United States by extending the linear pattern of decline among American Indians in the 1800s backwards to the precontact period. This method also produced an estimate of about 1.8 million. However, as Thornton (1988) points out, earlier declines in the population were not likely to have been linear, but steeper at the onset of contact.

Thus, Thornton recalculated, using Dobyns' depopulation ratios of 1/20 and 1/25, but changing the nadir population from 1930 Census counts to 1890–1900 estimates of the American Indian population. His rationale for doing so was evidence that the 1930 population was too large to be a correct nadir population (Thornton & Marsh-Thornton, 1981; Driver, 1968). Using this methodology produces an estimate between 5 and 6.2 million.

Mooney's estimate of precontact population size in the Southwest was 72,000 in New Mexico and Arizona. This would include Navajo, Apache, Pima, Papago, Pueblo, and other tribes (Ubelaker, 1976). An updated estimate by Ubelaker (1976) revises this number upward to 113,760. This doesn't give us any information specifically on the Navajo. Kunitz (1981) estimates that the Navajo numbered about 10,000 in 1864, and cites an earlier estimate of 2,000 Navajo in 1700. This early estimate, if true, would result in a fivefold increase in population in 164 years, or a doubling every 33 years.

The Navajo tribe certainly did not sustain losses of the same magnitude as many of the other tribes. The Navajo population has probably increased continuously from the sixteenth century onwards (Johansson, 1982). A number of factors probably contributed to the Navajo good fortune (Johansson & Preston, 1978). The Navajo resided in a remote area and had a low population density. These two factors limited European contact and the spread of communicable disease. The Navajo were also less sedentary than many other tribes, and as such, would have been less likely to contract diseases resulting from the accumulation of human waste. They may have had increased resistance to disease as well, since their diet was richer in animal proteins than their Hopi neighbors' (Johansson & Preston, 1978). Kunitz estimates that Navajo fertility in 1900 was actually lower than Hopi, but survival was higher, resulting in almost one extra child still living (Kunitz, 1983:32). The potential roles of cultural and economic adaptation and migration in the growth of the Navajo will be explored in a later section.

Ubelaker and others predict continued growth for the American Indian population for the foreseeable future. Though American Indians comprised less than one percent of the total U.S. population in 1980, they are one of, if not the, fastest growing minority in the country. Calculating recent growth rates for this population is almost as complicated as estimating the pericontact population, because of changing methodologies used by the Census Bureau and by the number of different agencies reporting data for American Indians. These details will also be discussed in a later section.

Socioeconomic Status

Despite the somewhat rosy picture painted by a demographic recovery, the American Indian has yet to participate in a social or economic recovery. Large gains were made by American Indians between the 1970 and the 1980 census in the areas of education and income (Snipp, 1989). However, as a group, they have the lowest per capita income and the highest unemployment rates. The median family income for Indians in 1979 was slightly higher ($13,724) than for African Americans ($12,598), but Indian families are larger. In 1980, 28.2% of American Indians were living below the poverty level, compared to 12.4% of all Americans, and the average family income was almost seven thousand dollars less (IHS, 1989). Only 55% of the population aged 25 and older were high school graduates, and only 7% were college graduates (IHS, 1989). These education statistics are also very similar to those for the African American population:

only 51% of blacks over age 25 had a high school diploma and 8.4% had four or more years of college in 1980 (Snipp, 1989).

It appears, however, that American Indians are making more rapid educational progress than the African American population. In 1970 only 22% of Indians over age 25 had completed 12 years of schooling, compared to 31.4% of blacks, but by 1980 a greater proportion of Indians had graduated from high school (Snipp, 1989). There were no differences in gains at the postsecondary level. Between Navajo men and women, however, there are large differences. In the late 1970s, almost twice as many women as men were in higher education (Shepardson, 1982).

Unemployment increased from 1970 to 1980 from 11.6% to 17.3% for Indian males, but the percentage not in the labor force declined during the decade from 36.6% to 30.4%, about the same amount as the increase in unemployment (Snipp, 1989). One-fourth of the Indian population (excluding Alaska Natives) did not have telephones, and one-fifth did not have public water in their dwellings (Snipp, 1989).

However dismal these statistics are, the statistics for the Navajo are even worse. Among Navajo families, almost half (47.3%) lived below the poverty level in 1979; median family income in 1980 was only $9,079, and only 34% of the adult population had completed high school (Navajo Nation, 1988). Only 52% of Navajo males were in the labor force; 22% of the families had no workers in 1979. Half the homes were without piped water, and 79% had no telephone (Navajo Nation, 1988).

Ethnographic Highlights

While it is beyond the scope of this project to include a detailed ethnography of the Navajo, some understanding of the culture is necessary to interpret the data presented. It is important to remember that, in any group, not every member will be adequately characterized by a general description of the culture. All cultures are dynamic, and as they evolve, some aspects are reinforced while other aspects simply become "old-fashioned." In the same way, each individual is a unique blend of situation and personal, as well as cultural, history. With this in mind, I shall attempt to outline some of the more salient features of the Navajo, as detailed in the ethnographic literature (Spencer & Jennings, et al., 1977; Kluckhohn & Leighton, 1962; Leighton & Kluckhohn, 1947; Terrell, 1970; Iverson, 1981; Harris, 1971; Downs, 1971; Locke, 1989).

The Navajo are newcomers relative to most of the other Amerindian groups represented in north and south America. They are an Athabascan group related to the Apache and other Indian groups in Canada and Alaska. Evidence of their presence in the Southwest can only be documented back to about 1500 A.D., with hints of Navajo occupancy possibly as early as 1100 to 1200 A.D. (Spencer & Jennings, et al., 1977; Terrell, 1970).

They were initially a hunter-gatherer group, organized into small bands, and maintained a system of patrilineal descent (Terrel, 1970). However, the Navajo were quick to selectively borrow material and social culture from neighboring Pueblos, and from the Spanish after their arrival. They learned weaving, agriculture, and animal husbandry, and incorporated Pueblo ceremonial ritual and myth into their own culture. Their current system of matrilineal descent was probably also borrowed from the Pueblos. These borrowed beliefs and practices, as well as more recent ones, are now firmly and uniquely into Navajo culture.

Two important aspects begin to emerge from this brief introduction to Navajo culture. First, the Navajo culture is extremely flexible and can incorporate new ideas or techniques into the preexisting culture (Lamphere, 1977). Recent examples of this ability include the pickup truck and the Pendleton blanket carried by a woman (Downs, 1971; Spencer & Jennings, et al., 1977). Often the pickup truck will have feathers tied to the rear view mirror, just as in the old days when feathers were carried by runners or tied on horses for speed and sureness. Second, the female principle is primary, as evidenced by the matrilineal, matrilocal familial system, property and inheritance patterns, and even in the language and religion of the people. Changing Woman, Spider Woman and Salt Woman are some of the most prominent figures in Navajo mythology. Even the four directions are characterized by women: Earth Woman [east], Mountain Woman [south], Water Woman [west], and Corn Woman [north]. Matrilocal residence is the norm, but Lamphere (1977) found a variety of living patterns on the Navajo reservation, including patrilocal, neolocal, and uxorilocal households.

Despite the emphasis on women, the husband is usually the formal head of the household, spokesman to outsiders, and primary wage earner. If a Navajo woman marries more than once, it is likely that later husbands will have less authority within the family (Downs, 1972). Even the word "family" is problematic in Navajo culture. For the man, the word family is most often used to refer to his family of origin, rather than his wife and children.

Navajo society is both group-dependent and individualistic. There is clearly a strong social pressure to conform to the Navajo way of life. Both historical and present conditions make interdependency imperative. However, in Navajo culture, it would be presumptuous for a man to speak for his wife regarding her thoughts or wishes even if he had certain knowledge of them, and vice versa. Likewise, parents acknowledge a child's individual belongings and give weight to his or her personal desires. Autonomy is encouraged when it does not threaten group survival or established patterns of interaction. Consensus rather than authoritarianism characterizes Navajo relations. Historically, many treaties signed by individual Navajo leaders were never binding to the tribe as a whole, simply because no one individual or even a group of individuals could claim the power to speak for all the Navajo.

The clan system defines relations and expectations of reciprocity among people. Ideally, mates are chosen from outside the clans of both mother and father, and some related clans. There are many clans (50–60), some formed when groups of various Pueblo Indians joined the Navajo. The clan serves as a wide resource base which can be tapped when one is far from home or in the event of illness or scarcity. Kinship terms dictate appropriate behavior. As a general rule, one may be easy or direct with consanguinal relatives, while shyness or indirectness is appropriate with affines. Age, sex, and marital status may modify rules for correct behavior. For example, direct communications between brother and sister are disrupted if the brother marries. A sister in need of assistance under these circumstances would approach her brother's wife, rather than approach her brother directly. This custom further buttresses the power of women in Navajo culture.

Age is a predictor of prestige and power, especially when coupled with numerous offspring, hard work and something to show for it, e.g., wealth or property. Wealth, to the Navajo, is primarily a family matter, rather than an individual circumstance, as there is strong pressure for a rich individual to spend generously on his family. A person with "too much" or who is stingy with his resources will be viewed with suspicion. The society's regard for wealth was one reason that the stock reduction program implemented in the 1930s was so unpopular. Both Levy (1964) and Downs (1971) have noted that the Navajo are very property conscious and acquisition-oriented. This acquisitiveness may also help to explain why the Navajos have been quick to adapt non-indigenous ways once their utility has been noted.

Children are highly valued in Navajo society (Leighton, 1947). The matrilineal, matrilocal system of descent makes children an asset, almost a necessity for women in old age.

This is especially true since spousal bonds tend to be weak, a common feature of matrilineal, matrilocal systems (Harris, 1971). Spousal bonds are weakened in two ways. First, although a man may marry and leave his mother's household, his obligations to her and to the offspring of his siblings do not cease with his leaving. He may be required to spend significant amounts of time or money in the maintenance of his mother's or sisters' households. This creates a conflict of competing demands over the allocation of resources between his family of origin and the family he has created by marriage.

Second, since the father in a matrilineal, matrilocal system can never control the assets of his children, and his sons will move away from him when they marry, it is not in his self interest to invest heavily in them, emotionally or financially. If domestic quarrels arise, it may simply be easier for him to return to his mother or sisters (Harris, 1971).

The matrilocal system does provide continuity and survival advantage in societies where the male is required to be either mobile or absent for extended periods of time, however (Harris, 1971; Lancaster, 1989). This has been the case for the Navajo in the past as a result of livestock dependence. Currently, the lack of development on the reservation and population pressures have forced men off the reservation to seek employment and have recreated a male-absent scenario. The extended family group of female kin (locally called "outfit") may also independently support high fertility in the face of tremendous economic problems. A woman may join the labor force without the usual concerns for childcare availability, since she has sisters, mother, aunts, and nieces in close proximity to care for her children, and her wages will benefit the whole group. Kunitz (1989) found that women living in these kin network systems were less likely to use contraceptives than other Navajo women (p. 184).

The Navajo seem to have little fear of dying, but an extreme fear of death itself. A death in a Navajo hogan traditionally necessitates abandonment of the dwelling. In the

Navajo belief system, there is no afterlife, and what remains of most individuals after death is a mean-spirited, vengeful ghost (*chindi*) who can harm the living if proper precautions are not taken. Navajos welcomed the arrival of hospitals and clinics on the reservation because they served as a place for the sick to die, and relieved the Navajo of much anxiety in dealing with the death of a relative. In former days, the task of burying a Navajo corpse often fell to a cooperative white trader. Interestingly, early white physicians on the Navajo reservation were not considered competent because their services were free. Navajos have traditionally equated worth with cost; the medicine men who charged the most were the most valued.

Most of Navajo ritual focuses on disease, in contrast to Pueblo ritual which focuses on rainfall and fertility (Kluckhohn & Leighton, 1962:238). Illnesses, both physical and mental, have their origins in the supernatural. Navajos are not troubled by a body/mind dichotomy. Disease or injury may be caused by excess, by failure to observe rituals or taboos, or by not being in harmony with the natural or the supernatural (gods, ghosts, or witches). Diviners and singers may be employed, alone or in conjunction with Western medicine, to bring the individual back into harmony with the group and with nature. As such, disease carries with it a social sanction. What has the sick person done or not done to cause this illness (Kluckhohn & Leighton, 1962)?

The Navajo belief in witchcraft is also a form of social sanction, and serves many of the same purposes outlined by Kai Erickson in *Wayward Puritans* (1966): to define and label deviant behavior within the group, to mark the group's boundaries, to discourage deviant behavior, and to promote group solidarity and unity. Nowadays, witch talk has subsided, but remains an undercurrent; it survives in oft-repeated stories, no matter how old, and legends passed on to future generations. Navajo daily life is filled with ritual and superstition.

Proselytizing by various religious groups among the Navajo was and still is fiercely competitive, but marginally successful. Compared to the Pueblos, who have incorporated Catholicism into their ritual practices, the Navajo were bombarded by many different faiths, each espousing their own theology, and all contrasting sharply with traditional Navajo beliefs. Many of these groups have operated schools or health clinics in conjunction with their religious activities, and have attempted to replace Navajo values with their own in the most vulnerable segments of the population, the children and the ill.

Perhaps the Mormons have been more successful than any of the other "white Christian" groups in winning converts. Both groups shared a past that was agricultural in orientation, and both had practiced polygyny. The Mormons believe that Indians are descendants of the lost tribe of Israel and were once destined to receive special blessings. At the end of 1989, there were 18,716 members of the Church of Jesus Christ of the Latter-day Saints (Mormons) on the Navajo Reservation, or approximately ten percent of the population (personal communication, Research Department, Church of Jesus Christ of Latter-day Saints). Whether these are active members, conforming to the precepts of the church, is unknown. Navajos may combine Western religion with traditional, native beliefs or with peyotism.

The Native American Church, a pan-Indian, peyote cult religion, has gained a large number of members and recognition, especially in the most rural areas. Terrell (1970) cites that approximately 20,000 Navajos were associated with the Native American Church. Terrell also notes that peyote use in religious ceremonies developed only after the stock reduction program of the 1930s. Peyote use on the reservation was banned from 1940 until the 1960s, but continued, surreptitiously or defiantly, nevertheless. Peyote ceremonies are curing rituals, much like traditional sings. In fact, Kunitz (1989) suggests that peyotism may be gaining in popularity because fewer singers are now available because of the long apprenticeship that is necessary. The peyote ceremony serves much the same purpose, and is less costly and much less time-consuming.

These then are the traditional views and values of the Navajo that are deemed important in understanding the data that will be presented. The Navajo made a seemingly favorable shift from a hunter-gatherer to a pastoral way of life, borrowing successfully from both the Pueblo and the Spanish. The transition to a wage-based economy is still in process, and has been uneven.

There is tremendous variability in life styles among the Navajo, especially among the young. Whether the Navajo world view will remain unchanged in its essential aspects is unknown. The reservation may be thought of as an island surrounded by a completely different culture. It is into this culture that the Navajo must now venture for a livelihood, just as the island resident must harvest from the ocean. Some of the characteristics of the Navajo are likely to be assets in this venture; others may be liabilities. Extending the island analogy briefly, we should remember that among reservations, the Navajo is the largest and perhaps best insulated from mainstream culture. If any reservation group will be able to retain its traditional culture amidst the ocean of Americana, it will most likely be the Navajo.

A brief discussion of important historical dates, presented below, completes the background information necessary for interpreting the data which follow.

Important Historical Dates

First contact with the Spaniards was recorded in 1626 and 1630. The direct effect of Spanish contact was probably minimal because the Navajo were spread out geographically and the terrain was so rough. The indirect effects were of enormous consequence, however. Conquest and occupation of various Pueblo groups along the Rio Grande sent refugees westward to the Navajo. Refugee migration increased substantially after the Pueblo Revolt of 1680, fueled by the fear that the Spaniards would return in vengeance (Terrell, 1970). It was during this time of amalgamation with the Pueblos that many of the Pueblo customs, such as weaving, were refitted to become uniquely Navajo.

The Spaniards also brought the sheep and horse into the realm of the Navajo. With these, the Navajo developed into one of the most skillful trading and raiding societies. They brought commerce and terror to the Americans, who were left to deal with the Navajo after the Spaniards finally departed.

The Spaniards and Mexicans bear some responsibility for the entrenched raiding behavior that the Americans encountered. It was both fashionable and practical to hold slaves in the territory of New Mexico during the eighteenth century. Navajo slaves were even favored. Up to and including the famous Kit Carson roundup of Navajos for the Long Walk, slave taking was a common occurrence. Much of the Navajo raiding was in retaliation for incursions into their territory, stealing women and children to be sold as slaves (Terrell, 1970).

Moreover, in fear of French occupation of their northern colonies, the Spaniards also had a policy of encouraging intertribal warfare and the taking of captives from tribes who traded with the French. The Spanish made few and shortlived attempts to catholicize the Navajo, and finally considered them hopelessly heathen (Kluckhohn & Leighton, 1962). The descendants of the few Navajo who were converted reside in the separate locations of Cañoncito and Puertocito and were called "the People who are enemies" by other Navajos (Kluckhohn & Leighton, 1962:36).

In 1846, the United States took control of the territory ceded by Mexico. Promising to control marauding Indians, they began to establish military posts and sent civilian agents to establish peace in the region. The period of the Civil War sent these activities into remission, and the Navajo intensified their raiding activities. After numerous treaties signed only by local headmen were broken, the government, ignorant of Navajo social organization, sent Kit Carson into Navajo territory to capture or kill Navajos and to plunder their homes, crops, and animals.

On March 6, 1864, the Long Walk of captured and surrendered Navajos and their animals began, commencing at Fort Defiance and ending at Fort Sumner, 300 miles southeast. The site was also called Bosque Redondo; the Navajo called it *Hweeldi*. Eight thousand Navajos were held in captivity there; an unknown number remained hidden in remote areas of Navajo territory. For more than four years the Navajo who survived and could not escape from *Hweeldi* remained in this alien and inhospitable place. The alkaline water made them sick; the crops they were forced to plant failed year after year; supplies and provisions were inadequate; and syphilis, dysentery and malnutrition were rampant. An estimated 2,000 Navajos died (Terrell, 1970).

Even though the provisions at Fort Sumner were grossly inadequate, it was finally the cost of provisioning them, and the Doolittle Commission's publicized report of the miserable conditions there, that forced a reconsideration of policy. There was some talk of relocating the Navajo to Oklahoma territory to make way for white settlers and to explore the rumors of mineral deposits in the Navajo territory. In the end, however, they were allowed to return to the area inside the four mountains and four rivers which, according to Navajo belief, had been given to them by First Woman of the Navajo (Terrell, 1970).

The treaty was made with the Navajos and the federal government, and signed on June 1, 1868. The Navajo headmen in captivity reluctantly, but forcefully, gave assurances that they spoke for the entire nation. Later that year, the People returned to a reservation of three and a half million acres, with almost no remaining dwellings, fruit trees, livestock, or cultivated land. There they began the painful process of rebuilding their lives and culture. Kluckhohn and Leighton (1962) contend that:

> One can no more understand Navajo attitudes—particularly toward white people—without knowing of Fort Sumner than he can comprehend southern attitudes without knowing of the Civil War. (p. 41)

The process of reconstruction was painful, hampered by weather, and complicated by delays in seed, implements, livestock, and rations the government had promised. A few rebellious Navajos began to conduct raiding parties again, but were promptly labelled witches by headmen who had been at Bosque Redondo and had no desire to be returned. These insurrectionists were soon mysteriously killed, and peace reigned. The vagaries, corruption, inefficiency, and ignorance of the Indian Bureau notwithstanding, the tribe slowly regained equilibrium, and began to flourish.

Considering their history, it is no wonder the Navajo have strong pronatalist beliefs. The experience at Bosque Redondo also fostered a sense of unity in the Navajo. They began to see themselves as the federal government saw them, as one people (Iverson, 1981).

From 1878 to 1886, there were five additions to the Navajo reservation, nearly quadrupling its size (Figure 2). However, as a result of climate, geography, and reliance on livestock, there were reports of overgrazing on the reservation as early as 1883. Overgrazing and soil erosion would become an even more urgent problem in the ensuing years.

In 1887, the Compulsory Indian Education Law was passed by Congress, and forced the Navajo to send their children away to boarding schools. The schools were run more like penal institutions than schools, and had as their spoken or unspoken agenda the eradication of Navajo culture and language. Navajo parents and children hated them for the

FIGURE 2
Successive Additions to the Navajo Reservation

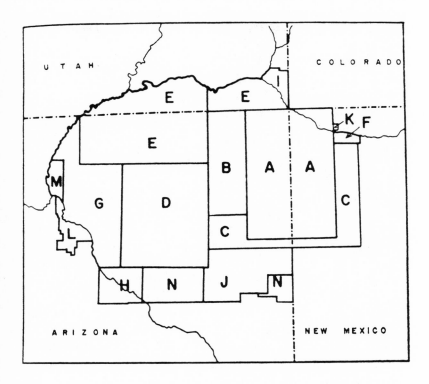

A: Treaty of June 1, 1868; B: Executive Order of October 29, 1878; C: Executive Order of January 6, 1880; D: Executive Order of December 16, 1882; E: Executive Order of May 17, 1884; F: Executive Order of April 24, 1886; G: Executive Order of January 8, 1900; H: Executive Order of November 14, 1901; I: Executive Order of May 15, 1905; and Act of March 1, 1933; J: Executive Orders of November 9, 1907, and January 28, 1908; K: Executive Order of December 1, 1913; L: Executive Orders of January 19, 1918, and May 23, 1930, and Act of June 14, 1934; M: Act of May 23, 1930; N: Act of June 14, 1934 (after Underhill 1963:149)

Source: Kunitz (1983)

emotional and economic trauma that resulted from the separation of child from parent in this farming society. When possible, the brightest children were hidden, and only the slaves from other tribes and orphans were sent to the boarding schools (Iverson, 1981). The tragic effects of boarding school practices would linger for many years, perhaps even into the present.

In 1912, New Mexico and Arizona gained statehood which made expansion of the reservation more difficult because the competing interests for land use in the area had official voice and more leverage than in the past. Neither state was eager to allot more land to the Indians.

The Metalliferous Minerals Leasing Act was passed in 1918. It permitted the Secretary of the Interior to lease Indian lands for mineral exploration and entitled the Indians to at least five percent of the royalties. However, the monies accruing to the Indians could be apportioned by Congress as they saw fit. With mineral leasing opportunities serving as the impetus, the Navajo Tribal Council was conceived. Membership was apportioned on the basis of population, a chairman and vice-chairman were elected, and the Council met for the first time on July 7, 1923 (Iverson, 1981).

In 1924, all Indians were granted U.S. citizenship. Some residing on allotment lands off reservations had previously obtained citizenship under the Dawes Act of 1887 (Iverson, 1981). The majority of Navajos, those residing in Arizona and New Mexico, would not be allowed to vote, however, until after court decisions in 1948.

The 1930s brought upon the Navajo not only the generalized conditions indicative of the Depression, but the personal deprivation of the stock reduction program. Although the need for such a program was undoubtedly urgent, the program was implemented hastily in 1933 without any advance attempts to educate the people. The underlying assumption of the program was that the land was severely eroded as a result of overgrazing, and that immediate and significant reduction in the number of livestock held by each family was essential. The Navajo way of life would be imperiled if the program was not implemented and strictly enforced. At least that was how John Collier, Commissioner of Indian Affairs, saw the problem; individual Navajos did not agree.

The Tribal Council faced a "catch-22" dilemma. If they did not approve the program, it would be forced on them anyway. Second, Collier held out the promise of relief programs and an extension of reservation lands in New Mexico if the program was approved. It was reluctantly approved by the Tribal Council, but additional lands were not forthcoming. Senator Dennis Chavez of New Mexico blocked Collier's efforts to add to the Navajo land base.

The stock reduction program created long-standing bitterness in the Navajo. It was unfair to smaller stock owners, and amidst the Depression economy, thousands of animals were senselessly slaughtered or sold for $1 per head. The stock reduction program was particularly hard on Navajo women; they were deprived of their traditional livelihood, and wage work was not generally available to them (Shepardson, 1982). The only positive results of the stock reduction program were that soil erosion was slowed and tribal unity was hastened.

The outbreak of World War II soon obscured the controversies of the stock reduction program and mandatory schooling. Approximately 3,600 Navajo served in the armed forces during the war. The most notable of these were the 420 Navajo Codetalkers who gained international fame by developing a code based on the Navajo language that the Japanese could not break. Another ten to twelve thousand men were employed in various war industries, in agriculture and in the railroad during the war years. Iverson (1981) states that over 50% of the population over age 19 were employed at this time.

As the war ended and the men returned home, they brought their experiences of the outside world into the reservation. Many of them could now clearly see the value of an education, and would become strong advocates of increased educational opportunities for Navajos in the future. However, the end of the war also brought a return of high unemployment which, coupled with raised expectations and continual shifts in federal policy and personnel, made this a dreary time. The Navajos hired their first legal counsel in 1947 to press their case under the Indian Claims Act passed in 1946, and to assist the tribe in dealing with increasing mineral extraction activities. It is important to remember that they still did not have voting privileges in New Mexico or Arizona at that time.

On August 5, 1954, perhaps one of the most important pieces of legislation affecting Indians was passed. It was known as the Transfer Act (PL 83-568) and transferred the responsibility for health care among Indians from the Bureau of Indian Affairs to the Public Health Service. In the late 1940s, health conditions on the Navajo reservation were abominable. Rates of tuberculosis were 13 times the U.S. rate, and over half the deaths occurred to children under age five (Iverson, 1981). After the transfer, new hospitals were built and additional physicians sent to the Navajo area. By demonstrating their ability to cure tuberculosis in a short period of time, physicians gained new respect on the reservation, and set the stage for improved relations with the Navajo. Mortality from a number of diseases began a steady decline after the inception of the Transfer Act.

In the 1960s, the Navajo spent most of their energies coping with newfound wealth from revenues obtained from oil and uranium reserves and trying to encourage development. In 1959, revenues from oil amounted to almost ten million dollars. Similarly, uranium revenues increased tenfold between 1950 and 1954. In 1963, the Navajo Tribal Council formally invited private capital investors onto the reservation.

In 1966, they allocated one million dollars to attract industry (Iverson, 1981). In a manner similar to Third World countries, they touted the advantages of cheap labor to be found on the reservation. They did not aggressively pursue the possibility of developing tribally-owned industry; rather, they focused on providing infrastructure and incentives for outside investment. They were fleeced in a couple of instances.

The tribe did, however, move to take full responsibility in the educational arena. In 1968, the Navajo Community College was founded, entirely under Navajo control. Classes began in January of 1969. The curriculum included college preparatory, vocational, and adult basic education courses. The College was open to all Navajos 18 years and older regardless of previous educational achievement, and tuition was free.

Two pieces of legislation enacted in the 1970s bolstered both the movement toward tribal control of health programs and provided additional monies for improved health care. In 1975, the Indian Self-Determination Act (PL 93-638) was passed giving tribes the option of manning and managing Indian Health Service programs. The Indian Health Care Improvement Act (PL 94-437) was passed in the following year to raise the level of health care among Indians, both reservation and urban, to that of the general population and to encourage greater Indian representation in the health professions.

The 1980s have brought continued improvements and modernization in the areas of health, education, transportation and communication (Navajo Nation, 1988; IHS, 1989). However, the current socioeconomic picture is still one of relative deprivation, as outlined earlier in this chapter.

Chapter **2**

THEORETICAL CONSIDERATIONS

A number of theoretical perspectives have been used to explain demographic changes, and the absence of change, in American Indian populations. Chief among these perspectives are: the theory of demographic and epidemiologic transition, social disorganization theory, minority group status, wealth flow, cultural lag, economic theories, and internal colonialism. One additional perspective, the biosocial model, has the potential to offer additional insights that complement the other perspectives.

Few of the theoretical perspectives are in direct conflict with other perspectives, but there are important differences in the policy implications deriving from them. There are also implied differences in the causes and consequences of demographic change. Each of the theoretical perspectives will be examined briefly in this chapter. In later chapters, as data are presented, I shall return to these perspectives and discuss their strengths, shortcomings, and linkages between them.

Demographic and Epidemiologic Transition

Thompson, and later Notestein, outlined a process by which human populations change in response to development (Weeks, 1989). High fertility and mortality rates characterize undeveloped societies, while the opposite is true of highly developed societies. The process of change from one to the other is known as the *demographic transition*. The theory specifies that, during the transition stage, mortality rates decline while birth rates remain high, setting the stage for rapid population growth. Modernization is the key element specified by this model as the cause of the demographic transition. Continued modernization provides the impetus for lowering fertility.

Berelson and others have attempted to specify threshold values of specific components of modernization that would trigger fertility decline (Mauldin & Berelson, 1978; Berelson, 1978). The underlying idea is that perhaps less than the totality of the macrostructural changes that occurred in the Industrial Revolution may be sufficient to lower fertility. The specific components of change that Berelson thought might indicate a "socioeconomic setting congenial to fertility reduction" include adult literacy, school enrollment, life expectancy, infant mortality rate, per capita GNP, percent of females aged 15–19 never married, and percent of labor force in non-agricultural sectors (Berelson, 1978). Most of these social factors will be evaluated in relation to American Indian fertility.

Demographic transition theory has been criticized for being bound to the cultural experiences of Western European countries and the United States as they modernized in the late 1800s and early 1900s as a result of the Industrial Revolution. However, Japan and some other non-Western countries have experienced the demographic transition more recently. Ansley Coale, in his now famous European Fertility History Project, found sufficient regional and temporal variation in the demographic transition in Europe in relationship to industrialization to question whether modernization alone could account for even the "classic" transition (Coale, 1973).

Coale and others have suggested that modernization was a sufficient, but not necessary, antecedent to transition, and attributed much of the transition to a process of secularization and cultural factors (Coale, 1973; Freedman, 1979). Freedman further suggests that "cultural groups often are related to fertility in ways that have not yet been explained by the general sociostructural factors central to transition theory" (Freedman, 1979). These cultural factors may have current relevancy in explaining the demographic patterns of American Indians in the U.S. and many Third World countries.

Its critics notwithstanding, demographic transition theory has gained wide acceptance as a useful general descriptive model of the dynamics of population change. It has not enjoyed specific explanatory or predictive power, especially with regard to the timing of population changes and wide regional variation within countries undergoing change (Coale, 1973; Teitelbaum, 1975).

Another valid, but infrequently cited criticism of transition theory is that it completely ignores the effects of migration (Nam & Philliber, 1984). Certainly a great deal of migration was occurring at the height of the Industrial Revolution in Europe, both internally to urban areas and internationally. Migration has been an historical way of dealing with population pressures without altering fertility patterns, at least for a generation or so. This is the theory of demographic change and response, outlined by Kingsley Davis in 1963. Davis felt that fear of poverty was not a good motivation for limiting fertility, as Malthus had suggested. Rather, he felt that it was the desire to improve one's status, or at least maintain it, that made people desire fewer children (Davis, 1963). However, as Weeks points out, it "assumes the individuals in question have already attained some status worth maintaining" (Weeks, 1989:79).

In the case of the Navajo, numerous tribal area expansions probably permitted continued population growth by periodically providing new settlement areas for tribal members. The land base for the Navajo began with an initial reservation of 3.3 million acres, and increased fivefold by the mid-1970s (Kunitz & Slocumb, 1976).

Navajo land acquisition has not abated. In 1986 alone, the tribe spent $19,141,700 and purchased 286,214 acres of tribal ranches. In 1987, the tribe controversially spent 13% of the total tribal revenues ($33,417,368) for the Big Boquillas ranch containing 729,532 acres (Navajo Nation, 1988).

Abdel Omran (1971) extended the demographic transition theory to include explanations for shifting causes of death that parallel changes in overall mortality rates. This theory is known as *epidemiologic transition*. Omran's extension of demographic transition theory postulates that causes of death will shift from a preponderance of infectious and parasitic diseases to a preponderance of "man-made" and degenerative diseases, as a society modernizes. In Western countries the shift occurred slowly, beginning before medical and organized public health interventions had any noticeable impact on mortality. In Europe, it took one to two hundred years to complete. Omran terms this the Western or Classic Model.

Two other types of transition may also occur: the Accelerated and the Delayed Models (Omran, 1971). Japan is the example cited by Omran of the Accelerated Model, where the birth rate fell rapidly after, or in conjunction with, declines in mortality. Abortion has played a primary role in lowering births in the countries included in the Accelerated Model.

The Delayed Model may be somewhat of a euphemism: an optimistic belief that countries that have experienced striking mortality declines will eventually bring their fertility under control to curb explosive population growth. In the Delayed Model particularly, medical and public health interventions have played a more significant role in rapidly reducing both absolute levels of mortality and deaths from specific causes. These interventions have largely been "imported" and do not reflect measures of internal development, modernization, cultural change, or the rising socioeconomic status of individuals within a country.

Broudy and May (1983) examined fertility and mortality patterns among Navajo Indians in the 1970s. They found high but possibly declining fertility, and shifts in mortality causes from high rates of infectious and parasitic diseases to high rates of "social pathology" diseases and increasing, yet low, rates of degenerative disease. Broudy and May suggest a somewhat uneven process of demographic and epidemiologic transition.

The life expectancy and crude death rates of the Navajo suggest that they have entered Omran's last stage of epidemiologic transition, that of the degenerative and "man-made" diseases, as well as the last stage of demographic transition. But fertility rates and the fact that pneumonia and influenza was the fifth leading cause of death in the Broudy and May (1983) study suggest the earlier stages of both transition theories. Additionally, the fact that social pathologies greatly exceeded degenerative disease mortality led the authors to conclude that some social disorganization theory must be included to account for effects of rapid and uneven modernization.

Rogers and Hackenberg (1987) believe that epidemiologic transition theory has several major short-comings. First, it may mask the interaction between chronic and infectious disease. Second, it cannot account for recent declines in such chronic diseases as hypertension and ischemic heart disease. Third, and possibly most important, "social pathology" deaths are combined with degenerative disease in Omran's conceptual framework. Moreover, the authors point out that the relationship between mortality and age, sex, and ethnicity have changed in the United States since the theory was elaborated (Omran 1982, 1983). For example, the elderly have made more substantial health gains in recent years than the young. Rogers and Hackenberg (1987) propose a new stage, termed the "hybristic" stage, to account for the rise and fall of mortality directly linked to individual behaviors or lifestyle. The term "hybristic" (or hubristic) refers to excessive self-confidence or arrogance. The Greeks used the word *hubris* to refer to the sin of believing one was a god.

Since Navajo mortality patterns are closely tied to behavior patterns, especially in males, and reductions in mortality are not likely to be achieved through medical advances, viewing epidemiologic transition through Rogers' and Hackenberg's extension of Omran's theory may provide additional insight. Rogers and Hackenberg do not address diseases or deaths produced or exacerbated by collective behaviors and lifestyle such as air and water pollution, other environmental exposures, or religious, racial or political intolerance. As such, additional extensions of Omran's theory may be necessary.

Internal Colonialism Theory

Stephen (1987) found evidence of declining, yet still elevated fertility rates among the Navajo. She used multivariate analysis to attempt to explain the underlying cause of extant high fertility in Navajos. The competing theoretical perspectives of modernization/assimilation and internal colonialism were tested, and little evidence was found to support the notion that modernization or assimilation had lowered fertility. Instead, Stephen attributes her findings to the existence of a system of internal colonialism, which does not predict that fertility rates of the Navajo will converge with those of whites as long as they remain a peripheral group.

The internal colonialism argument may be summarized as follows: Reservations are really Third World countries. They export labor and natural resources to the core area and import manufactured products which they cannot afford (Johansson, 1984). Poverty, low educational attainment, and the participation of children in the economy provide no incentive to lower fertility, and may provide positive incentives to keep fertility high. Thus, until Indians gain control over their economic destiny, they will continue to prefer large families. Johansson points out that a preference for large families as an antidote to poverty and political vulnerability will, in the end, only perpetuate the cycle of poverty and associated social factors, making the population as or more vulnerable than in the first place (Johansson, 1984).

Kunitz (1981), while not disputing epidemiologic transition theory in general, suggests that the Navajo may never have experienced the "pandemic" stage that Omran postulates, and that demographic comparisons between the Navajo and Hopi suggest patterns sufficiently different to preclude generalized conclusions about transition. Kunitz (1981) also explores the hypothesis that continued high fertility among the Navajo can be explained by internal colonialism. Kunitz notes that Navajos have become increasingly dependent on unearned income; Lamphere (1974) also notes the persistence of the welfare economy among the Navajo. The importance of livestock has diminished. Second, in the employment sectors, more Navajos are in the public service sector than other groups. The largest industries on the reservation are education and public administration. Third, the economic development that has occurred has not been a gradual building of the economy, but a boom/bust type of development.

Kunitz further ties the marginal economic circumstances of Navajos with an extended kinship system and low rates of contraceptive use leading to high fertility. The large, extended family is still useful to the Navajo, because jobs are uncertain and income must be obtained from a variety of sources. The family serves as a way to redistribute resources that may fluctuate by season or number of family members employed.

Wealth Flow Theory

Caldwell (1982) has formulated a theory of fertility decline that focuses on intrafamily dynamics as well as the larger social and economic system. He postulates that opportunities for wage labor and mass education begin to erode the traditional family mode of production, and to change the family structure itself from a rigid obligation system based on age, sex and relationship to a more egalitarian structure. These changes eventually erode the authority of the family patriarch and create a situation where children are viewed as a net disadvantage. The family's wealth begins to flow in the direction of the children, rather than from young to old. Having many children reduces the quality of the life of the elder generation, and becomes too costly.

Caldwell, unlike many other demographers, emphasizes the importance of intrafamily dynamics. External conditions may favor low fertility, but until relations within the family change, fertility will remain high and continue to be perceived as advantageous, such as in Islamic countries and in sub-Saharan Africa (Caldwell, 1982:229).

Caldwell's approach also differs from other demographic approaches to fertility decline in that he believes it is important to explain stable high fertility first, before trying to explain a decline. He believes that family planning programs (e.g., the availability of contraceptives) cannot initiate decline, although they may accelerate a decline that has already begun. He suggests that it is a mistake to interpret demographic change by demographic indicators, and to predict changes in Third World demographies by economic indicators.

Figure 3 outlines the process of destabilization of the traditional family that Caldwell sees as the impetus for declining fertility in Third World countries. He notes that mass education is more important in the Third World than it was in the West.

FIGURE 3
Antecedents to Fertility Decline in Third World Countries
(Adapted from Caldwell)

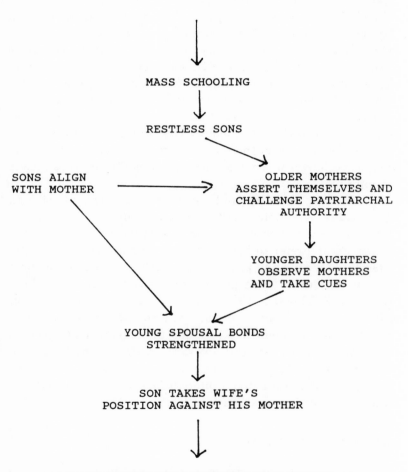

MASS SCHOOLING

RESTLESS SONS

SONS ALIGN
WITH MOTHER

OLDER MOTHERS
ASSERT THEMSELVES AND
CHALLENGE PATRIARCHAL
AUTHORITY

YOUNGER DAUGHTERS
OBSERVE MOTHERS
AND TAKE CUES

YOUNG SPOUSAL BONDS
STRENGTHENED

SON TAKES WIFE'S
POSITION AGAINST HIS MOTHER

OLDER GENERATION BECOMES SUBORDINATE
MULTIGENERATION HOUSEHOLD WEAKENED
FAMILIAL MODE OF PRODUCTION WEAKENED

Cultural Lag Theory

Some researchers argue that American Indians are just like mainstream Americans, only at some earlier point in time. For example, educational attainment in 1970 was comparable to that of white males in 1950 (Sorkin, 1976). Only in 1930 did the majority of white Americans reside in urban areas; in 1980, 49% of Indians resided in urban areas. These arguments predict that, as for many immigrant groups, time will eventually erase economic and social distinctions between American Indians and mainstream Americans. Sowell (1981) argues that blacks, Hispanics, and Indians have been so isolated from the mainstream of American life that it makes sociological sense to view them as if they were recent immigrants.

In fact, fertility and mortality patterns of African Americans, Hispanics, and American Indians are different from those of other Americans; they also differ from each other. Some prefer to believe that these patterns are simply associated with being poor, rural or urban, and that cultural factors unique to each group are really irrelevant. Others (Stanley & Thomas, 1978; MacAndrew & Edgerton, 1969; Mohatt, 1972) point to the warrior lifestyle and the preservation of traditional values underlying demographic differences between Indians and whites. This cultural explanation is plausible enough when applied to Indians, but it does not explain demographic differences between whites and other ethnic groups, such as blacks.

Biosocial Perspective

Yet another model for understanding patterns of fertility and parental investment in offspring comes from the biosocial perspective. This is an evolutionary-based model, and underlying this perspective is the belief that reproductive decisions, like other decisions, are evolved interactive strategies. They are decisions made at the juncture between culture and ecology, between opportunity and cost, and between micro- and macro-level phenomena. Those who advocate this perspective dismiss explanations such as modernization for low fertility as simplistic, ethnocentric and tautological: sweeping generalizations that do not offer genuine explanations of behavior.

The biosocial perspective is thus a critique of previous explanations, and a synthesis of a number of area studies in tandem with an evolutionary-based framework. This framework centers around the idea that humans have evolved to maximize reproductive success within the constraints of their environment through the proximate variables of social competition and learning (Turke, 1989). A number of key points and predictions from the biosocial perspective, especially those which may prove relevant to Navajo fertility patterns, follows.

The extended helplessness of human infants requires intensive care and provisioning for several years before any returns on the investment made by the parents can possibly be realized. The cost of successfully provisioning children has necessitated that humans become concerned with and adept at acquiring resources (Lancaster, 1983).

In societies where the child's or the parent's survival is in jeopardy, parental investment is likely to be different than in societies where child survival is more certain and resources are more abundant (Harpending, Draper & Pennington, 1990). For example, Scheper-Hughes (1985) found that mothers in a Northeast Brazil shantytown delay bonding with, and sometimes even naming, their infants until it appears that they will survive. Infants who exhibit weakness or lack of vitality are allowed to die "a mingua," by neglect. The epidemiology of spontaneous abortion, abandonment and infanticide also point to scarcity in the present coupled with optimism for the future as providing a high risk climate for fetuses and infants (Wasser & Isenberg, 1986; Wasser, 1990).

Delayed childbearing may also be a response to this type of scenario.

But, under conditions of long-term scarcity with no prospect for improvement and high infant mortality independent of parental care factors, such as those found by Scheper-Hughes (1985), the optimal strategy may be to have many children, but selectively invest in those who show the most promise (specific to the culture) of succeeding. Child spacing is one of the few ways these parents can influence child survival (Lancaster & Lancaster, 1987).

Parents with more resources could easily jeopardize their status by having too many children. Instead, they may adopt a strategy of having fewer children, and investing more heavily in each one. These investments go beyond those needed for survival, and may include preventive health care, education, travel and other "cultural" experiences. These investments may never benefit the parents directly, but they enable the child to be well-situated in the job and marriage market in early adulthood. In summary, the parents, by pursuing a higher quality life for themselves, are actually in a better position to achieve social and economic success, and to pass these on to their children. The benefits the offspring receive maximize the probability of their own (ergo their parents') reproductive success.

Where resources come from and how they are accessed depend on both the physical environment and on the cultural practices within the infrastructure of a given society. In Western, industrialized nations, access to resources is primarily through employment opportunities, available to both males and females with the requisite education. Women in Western societies may limit their fertility in order to take advantage of these opportunities for themselves and for their children. Divorce may also be higher as women have access to resources independent of men. In other societies, resources are most easily obtained through a cooperative network of people, usually relatives. As Handwerker points out:

> To the extent that material well-being can be created and maintained through personal relationships, children will be important sources of income flows. (Handwerker, 1986:15)

High fertility in these societies may be encouraged in a number of ways. First, opportunities for women to work in the formal sector economy are usually limited, thereby limiting their independent access to capital formation. Second, the cost of raising individual children is normally borne by a group larger than the nuclear family (Turke, 1989), making the task of having a large family less onerous than it would be under Western, nuclear family conditions. The cost of raising children in Western societies falls almost exclusively on the parents. Third, cultural and religious disincentives for limiting family size often complement the economic disincentives.

Another key tenet of the biosocial perspective is that the male choice of a reproductive strategy may depend upon the choices made by women in a given society (Lancaster, 1989). The reproductive strategies chosen by men and women are a result of biological, environmental, and macro-structural conditions. These strategies could maximize the number of surviving children for each, but conflict with the strategy pursued by the opposite sex. The biosocial model suggests that reproductive success is dependent on two types of activities: mating opportunities and parental investment. Time, cost, and energy spent in one activity curtail resources available for the other. The greatest share of parental investment is usually born by the mother. A successful pregnancy can be wasted if the infant fails to survive. Thus, a woman may forego mating opportunities during times of intense parenting demands since her activities and attentiveness are certain to impact child well-being and survival.

The activities of the father may or may not contribute to the child's well-being, depending on the abundance or scarcity of resources in the environment, and the father's access to those resources. A man who has limited or unpredictable access to resources may perceive (correctly) parental investment as a somewhat futile activity in comparison with the opportunity to pursue additional mating opportunities (Pennington & Harpending, 1988). A large segment of the African American population of the United States offers a glimpse of this strategy. Chronic unemployment, high mortality, low educational attainment, discrimination and prejudice, and aspects of our social welfare policies marginalize the black male to the point that the contributions he is able to make toward the well-being of his offspring are often negligible. The resultant high rate of illegitimate births and continued father absence from black households attests to the presence of this strategy.

In response to Caldwell's intergenerational wealth flow theory, biosocial theorists disagree that wealth flows upward in pre-transition societies and downward in modern societies. Instead, they suggest that wealth generally flows downward under conditions of both high and low fertility. By the time children are able to make net positive contributions to the household, they leave to create their own households. Turke (1989) argues that, because of our motivation for the reproductive success of ourselves and close kin, that wealth flows from non-reproductive to reproductively active individuals. A number of studies cited by Turke (1989) support this hypothesis in societies where kin interaction is common. The desire for help from children in old age, an often quoted reason for having many offspring, may be more wishful fantasy than actual fact, Turke (1989) suggests.

However, Turke has been criticized as having misread Caldwell, as being too reductionist himself, and for relying too heavily on sources that support his hypothesis while ignoring sources that refute it (Fricke, 1990). Nevertheless, both Turke and Caldwell predict similar outcomes for post-transition societies.

Biosocial theorists generally agree with other theoretical perspectives that once a transition from high to low fertility has begun, it is irreversible unless major changes occur in the distribution of resources. However, they explain this, not by the linear reasoning that modernization is inevitable and always accompanied by low fertility, but by our inheritance of a proclivity for social competition. Once some parents begin to limit fertility and invest more in their offspring, social competition forces other parents to follow, if their children are to become successful.

Most American Indian tribes have been and remain resource-limited. Perhaps their extant high fertility in light of dramatic declines in mortality reflects an evolutionary adaptation that continues to optimize the number of children in the next generation with limited resources available for each offspring. However, in contrast with poor African Americans and Hispanics, Indians do benefit from free health services and other government subsidies, so that basic needs can be met without having to pay the full cost of obtaining them outside the reservation area. These conditions probably are reflected in lower infant mortality rates for Indians. Whether, and under what conditions, these free subsidies lead to higher fertility is unknown. The type and amount of most available subsidies would seem to have little effect on increasing the competitiveness or social desirability of the individuals receiving them.

Both African American and Navajo populations have high illegitimacy rates and high unemployment rates for males. These cultures are both matrifocal, either overtly or de facto, and there are considerable differences in the reproductive strategy of each sex. A support network of female kin helps to reduce the individual burden of childrearing. Matrifocality has provided a pronatalist setting; differences in culture and access to resources have produced different adaptive fertility patterns in black and Navajo women. Navajos have continued a high fertility pattern. African

American women have lowered their individual fertility, but shortened the length between generations, as we shall see in Chapter 4. The biosocial perspective has the potential to illuminate these and other fertility patterns, and to synthesize economic and cultural theories that have traditionally been viewed as competitive.

Sex Ratio Theory

Another perspective that may be grouped with biosocial theory, although it is not usually part of that discourse, is the sex ratio theory developed by sociologist Marcia Guttentag. According to this theory:

> ... the number of opposite-sex partners potentially available to men or women has profound effects on sexual behaviors and sexual mores, on patterns of marriage and divorce, childrearing conditions and practices, family stability, and certain structural aspects of society itself. (Guttentag & Secord, 1983:9)

A shortage of women creates intense competition among men for mates, and gives women a certain amount of advantage in the interpersonal realm. To compensate for this imbalance in the dyad, men, who almost always hold the structural power in society, limit the freedoms of women. These limitations may take official form, such as marriage, divorce, and property laws. Or they may be less formal sanctions regarding dress and behavior, for example. In societies where women are scarce, they are too precious to be allowed certain freedoms. They are viewed romantically, and idealized as wives, mothers, or sweethearts. Monogamous commitment is the norm, and virginity is prized.

When women predominate, another scenario results. Sexual mores are relaxed, and with abundant mating opportunities, males become more reluctant to make a monogamous commitment. Women become the dependent partner in the dyadic relationship because of limited alternatives other than being alone. In this stressful and unfavorable predicament, women may work to reduce their dependency on men. The feminist movement is an example of this attempt to redress inequalities of social exchange, and Guttentag and Secord attribute the rise of this movement to an overabundance of marriageable age women in the 1960s.

Sex ratio imbalances create their effects by disrupting the symmetry of social power between males and females. Two kinds of power are at stake here. One is the interpersonal, or dyadic power, resulting from the interaction of an individual couple. The second is the structural, macro-level power: to create and enforce laws, to exercise authority, to dictate policy, to influence. Structural power has historically been in the hands of men, but as women move into the work force and reduce their dependence on men as they have in a number of post-industrial societies, enormous shifts in the status quo of structural power can be expected to occur, and may in fact be occurring.

One question of interest here is how the sex ratio theory relates to a matrilineal, matrilocal society such as the Navajo. There is no concept of joint property between spouses among the Navajo, and the most prestigious deities are women (Kluckhohn & Leighton, 1962). Women are the real owners of the traditional means of production, sheep and land and looms for weaving, in this society. Furthermore, the sex ratio at birth is presently lower than that of the U.S.

Predictions from Theory

Each of these theories specifies a certain set of circumstances which produces or is associated with a particular demographic pattern. Some of the predictions are specific; others less so. With the exception of Berelson's attempt to quantify the socioeconomic characteristics that could produce a demographic transition, none of the theories tell us how much of a decline in mortality or an increase in development, for example, will produce the specified effect. They are equally vague with respect to timing, that is, when an effect can be expected after some other condition has been achieved. With this in mind, let us proceed to see what each of these theories predicts for the Navajo, and how they might be related to each other.

In general, all the theories predict that Navajo demographic patterns will converge with those of the United States after the sociocultural and economic patterns converge. Convergence does seem to be occurring in some arenas, but greater divergence is occurring in others. Not only that, but some aspects of larger American society seem to be converging with Navajo patterns, not vice versa. A particularly good example of this phenomenon is the rapid growth of single childbearing in the United States. Obviously, more specificity is needed. Is change inevitable? Which aspects of the totality are more important? How do variables relate to or interact with each other? Are endogenous or exogenous factors more important? How long does it take to observe demographic change effects after social or other demographic changes have taken place?

Taking each theoretical perspective in turn, general predictions will be identified; where possible specific hypotheses will be stated. As the data are presented in Chapters 4 through 7, they will be linked to the relevant theoretical perspectives, with an attempt to identify the assets and liabilities of each perspective. The concluding chapter will return to these perspectives in an attempt to synthesize, and suggest directions for future research. The nature of these vital statistics data do not permit extensive formal testing of hypotheses.

The only theory that addresses mortality specifically is the demographic and epidemiologic transition. The rest concern themselves with fertility decline or family structure. Concerning the demographic transition, as it was outlined and embellished, Navajo mortality rates have already declined to low levels. The remainder of demographic transition theory involves lowered fertility: whether and when it will occur, and if so how much of a decline will be observed. One problem with this theory is its vagueness. Supporters of transition theory use time trends for whole nations; detractors point to local diversity. Both appear to be true. A second problem is that the effects of migration on fertility and mortality are ignored.

Berelson's attempt to quantify modernization and specify the important components of fertility decline are admirable. His thresholds undoubtedly produce positive correlation coefficients using cross-national whole nation data. Whether they would work as well on a case by case basis, using smaller population groups is doubtful. In the case of the Navajo, Berelson's predictions of the conditions that produce a decline in fertility are obviously misspecified.

By including Omran's extension of demographic transition, we will be able to examine changes over time in causes of death. It may be necessary to question some of Omran's assumptions in terms of the categories of death characteristic of modern and transitional societies. Why, for example, would a smoking-related cause of death be grouped with degenerative diseases and alcohol-related deaths with "man-made" causes?

Davis' theory of demographic change and response essentially predicts that migration will be the first option in coping with population pressures. When these options are exhausted, fertility will decline. The Navajo have faced continual population pressure, straining the resources of the land since the inception of the reservation in 1868. They were fairly successful in gaining additional land by executive order until the 1920s. The tribe's new strategy seems to be to purchase outright large tracts of land that are for sale. The Navajo are also free to leave the reservation and settle wherever they please. However, those who do leave are certain to be different in many respects from those who remain. Simply comparing the fertility of the two groups is not likely to be an adequate test of theory.

The same problem confronts the test of internal colonialism. Internal colonialism predicts that fertility will remain high until endogenous development occurs. Navajo fertility is high and the reservation, despite recent attempts, is still woefully undeveloped by modern standards. To test this theory adequately, we might wish to compare metropolitan and non-metropolitan fertility among all Indians, or design a case-control study of Navajo women living on the reservation compared to urban Navajo. However, factors other than internal colonialism might just as easily explain differences, if any were observed. A final note concerning internal colonialism: the cost of recent land acquisition could be reinforcing the internal colonialism pattern, if one exists. As the tribe chooses to invest money in land that could otherwise be invested in development, they may be postponing real development and clinging to pastoralism.

Cultural lag theory, made plausible by Sowell when applied to African Americans, doesn't seem to have much relevance to Navajos. In Sowell's book *Ethnic America* (1981), American Indians are notably absent; only immigrant groups are considered. Immigrants today overwhelmingly move to large urban areas. Most Navajos are not moving to cities at all, and the ones who are seem to be settling primarily in smaller cities adjacent to or near the reservation. Sowell points out that while upward mobility or progress is not inevitable, it has been observed in every immigrant group coming to the United States. He points out that Jews and slaves got a better deal in the United States than they did elsewhere. Perhaps the same can be said for the American Indians in this country compared to those in Latin America. This speculation is merely a digression, however, and the fact remains that cultural lag is not an explanation so much as it is a description.

Wealth flow theory has a great deal of relevance to this investigation. The main problem here is that Caldwell assumed a pre-existing patriarchal social structure that eventually disintegrated. Do the same predictions apply when the pre-existing structure is matrifocal? Caldwell suggests that a high infant mortality rate is a quantitative indicator that there is still an emphasis on the needs of the older generation, that there has not been a change in the emotional flow which is a precursor to the change in the wealth flow. The fact that Indian and Navajo infant mortality rates are now quite low either refutes Caldwell's notion or supports it by suggesting that fertility decline and changes in family structure are imminent.

The biosocial perspective predicts that fertility will remain high and single childbearing and childraising will be prominent features of a society as long as males do not have the resources to invest in their children. The matrilineal form of Navajo society may accentuate this pattern. While the tribe is acquiring additional land, women who favor the traditional sheepgrazing, pastoral economy will be in control of it. Prospects for wage labor on the reservation will be suppressed, and males will continue to be marginal or seek off-reservation work and be absent from the household. Women, in order to survive, will cling to their matrilineal kinship networks which favor high fertility, and thus the cycle is perpetuated.

Sex ratio theory may also be applicable to the Navajo since there are fewer males at birth, and since high mortality characterizes the early adult years of men. However, this theoretical perspective also needs to be refitted to the Navajo matrifocal family structure. It is unclear what specific structural power men hold in Navajo society, and how that power relates to women.

In summary, we will be looking for explanations for extant high fertility in the Navajo, as well as some of the patterns of childbearing which differ substantially from those of the larger society. For example, how is it that birth outcomes of this socioeconomically disadvantaged group are so favorable? There is also the question of changing mortality patterns and the extreme survival disadvantage of males.

The next step is to examine the quality and limitations of these data for the purposes of analysis.

Chapter **3**

METHODOLOGIC ISSUES

The data for this investigation come from three primary sources: 1) computer tapes from the Indian Health Service (IHS) containing vital statistics from 1983 to 1986 for all Indians in the U.S. as coded on birth and death certificates and submitted to the National Center for Health Statistics (NCHS); 2) publications from the Bureau of the Census; and 3) special studies and population estimates produced by the Indian Health Service and the Navajo tribe.

Vital statistics data were analyzed using SAS software, rates were hand calculated, and multiple decrement life tables were produced using software developed by Eun Sul Lee at the University of Texas Health Science Center, School of Public Health.

Matching numerator (vital statistics) data with denominator (Census, Indian Health Service and tribal population estimates) data for the purpose of calculating rates is always problematic when dealing with less than the totality of the population of the United States. Even then, using intercensal estimates by age group may produce errors if there have been shifts in fertility or mortality patterns since the last census, and these changes have not been incorporated in the estimates. Some of the general problems confronting an investigation of fertility and mortality in American Indians are discussed below in further detail.

Numerator Considerations

Race identification of birth and death certificates depends on several factors that vary across and within states. The knowledge of the person completing the certificate is critical. In some cases a physician completes the entire certificate; in cases of death, a funeral director may complete the social information. This individual's knowledge of the family is indispensable for accurate coding on the certificate. Indians who live and die on a reservation are more apt to be coded correctly than Indians living in either urban or rural areas outside reservation areas. Physicians and funeral directors in the region of the Navajo reservation are sensitive to these issues; the quality of race and ethnic information on birth and death certificates for this population is apt to be better than for many other Indian groups.

In New Mexico, unattended deaths are under the jurisdiction of the Office of the Medical Investigator (OMI). Further, all suspicious deaths are autopsied. Since many Indian deaths are accidental, especially in the younger age groups, we can expect that these deaths will have accurate ethnicity coding and accurate cause of death codes as well. In fact, a review of New Mexico Indian suicide deaths from 1980 to 1987 revealed that 71% of the certificates had been signed by OMI personnel, 23% were autopsied, and 90% had toxicology reports (Van Winkle & May, 1986).

Some states with large Hispanic populations use surname as an indicator of Hispanic ethnicity, and attempt to identify Hispanics separately on birth and death certificates. Many American Indians share surnames with Hispanics as well as phenotypic characteristics, so that a certifier who noted only the appearance or surname of an individual might classify American Indians as Hispanics. Many Pueblo Indians in New Mexico and Indians elsewhere in the western part of the U.S. have a Spanish surname.

Tribal identity is not typically recorded on birth or death certificates. New Mexico does code tribe, however; Arizona encourages the recording of tribe, but does not code it at present. Thus, calculating vital rates by tribe depends on assumptions of tribe from place of residence, and may be very unreliable. Other factors related to cultural practices may differentially affect the quality of the numerator, especially in cause of death coding. Autopsy is relatively rare among older southwestern Indians. We expect to find a significant proportion of deaths in older age groups to be classified as deaths due to senility and ill-defined causes. Older individuals may also not know their date of birth, causing age misclassification on the death certificate.

Proximity and sensitivity to American Indians may help ensure correct race and ethnic coding on the death certificate, but it may introduce bias in the determination of cause of death. For example, the publicity surrounding Indian alcoholism and suicide may make it more likely that a physician will look for and find evidence of this sort in the patient's history or circumstances of death. A non-Indian death may not be given this careful scrutiny. The result may be an exaggeration of differences between Indians and other groups.

Nevertheless, by choosing to focus specifically on the Navajo reservation area, many of the numerator and denominator problems can be minimized. A review of missing service unit codes in the mortality file by state and county of residence revealed zero missing codes for Navajo reservation counties in Arizona and one missing code for McKinley county in New Mexico. For other areas, service unit codes were missing in a majority of cases in the file.

The all U.S. Indian comparison group must be viewed in light of the above caveats, and with the understanding that the statistics presented represent the central tendency of a highly diverse group of people. Living conditions vary tremendously from South Dakota to Oklahoma, from upstate New York to North Carolina, and from Alaska to Florida.

Denominator Considerations

Census counts of American Indians in 1980 compared to 1970 were 70% higher, 1,364,033 compared to 792,730 (Table 1). This represents an approximate 7% average annual growth rate, virtually a demographic impossibility since immigration of American Indians to the U.S. is not a major consideration. A similar, but smaller, error of closure occurred between the 1960 and 1970 census.

TABLE 1

American Indians Enumerated
in Decennial Censuses, 1900–1980

Census Year	Count	Annual Percent Change From Earlier Census
1900	237,196	—
1910	276,927	1.7%
1920	244,437	−1.2%
1930	343,352	4.1%
1940	345,252	0.1%
1950	357,499	0.3%
1960	523,591	4.6%
1970	792,730	5.1%
1980	1,364,033	7.2%

Source: PC80-1-B1, General Population Characteristics, United States Summary, Table 40.

The most obvious explanation for the observed discrepancies is improved coverage of the American Indian population in succeeding censuses. However, the sheer magnitude of the error of closure and the patterns of inconsistencies by age and by region of the country suggest simple undercounting in previous censuses is not a completely adequate explanation. Passel and Berman (1986) believe that significant and increasing numbers of young adults have begun reporting American Indian race and ancestry since the 1960s, particularly in traditionally non-Indian areas. This growth by "recruitment" is not a major consideration in Arizona and New Mexico.

Other limitations relevant to this study include the paucity of census data by detailed age and sex categories for specific tribes, and the presentation of tables containing non-Indians living within tribal reservation areas. Other information presented is based on samples. The sampling methodologies used by the Census Bureau may produce statistics with larger errors for American Indians than for other groups.

Over the years, and depending on the agency collecting information, Indians have been classified variously by appearance, blood quantum, tribal membership, government-recognized, and self-identified. No one definition has gained universal acceptance. Various tribes and the Indian Health Service regularly prepare population estimates in the detail required and for intercensal years, but definitions of eligibility for inclusion in the data base vary. For example, tribes may count members on tribal rolls who reside in urban areas far away from the reservation, and may not count Indian spouses from other tribes who do reside on the reservation. The Indian Health Service counts only those meeting the eligibility requirements for receiving health care, which is generally official membership in a federally recognized tribe and residence in particular counties or states. These methods differ substantially from those of the Census Bureau, where race and ethnicity are subjective choices made by the person being enumerated; no objective criterion must be met for a person to declare him/herself as American Indian.

Intercensal estimates prepared by the Indian Health Service are limited by the methodology currently employed to produce these statistics. The IHS simply carries forward the age and sex proportions from the most recent census, almost five years old at the midpoint of this study period. This shortcoming is most severe at the smaller geographic levels, such as the service unit.

Service units are IHS administrative boundaries within the reservation (Figure 4). Service unit estimates by age and sex were obtained from the Navajo Area Indian Health Service (NAIHS), but they were produced by multiplying age and whole tribe by estimates of the total population of each service unit. For this reason, only service unit data that would be least affected by the intercensal estimation method are presented, such as general fertility rates and sex ratios at birth.

A worthwhile project for future research would be to develop more sophisticated estimates and projections utilizing 1990 Census data as the baseline. Because of differences in development among service units, these data would be of value in searching for causal explanations for differences observed within the reservation.

The Navajo nation lies in portions of three states and ten counties. Various other Indian tribes also reside in these counties, including the Apache, Hopi, Ute and Pueblo. Some of these groups may be included in both the numerators and denominators of rates presented in this study. In addition to what is locally known as "big Navajo," there are three other bands of Navajo (Cañoncito, Ramah, and Alamo) residing in New Mexico. Thus, the Navajo tribe per se does not inhabit a "census-definable" region; Navajos reside in four separate non-contiguous locations. The Navajo population is also served by two Area Offices of the Indian Health Center.

FIGURE 4

Service Unit Boundaries and Location of Hospitals and Clinics

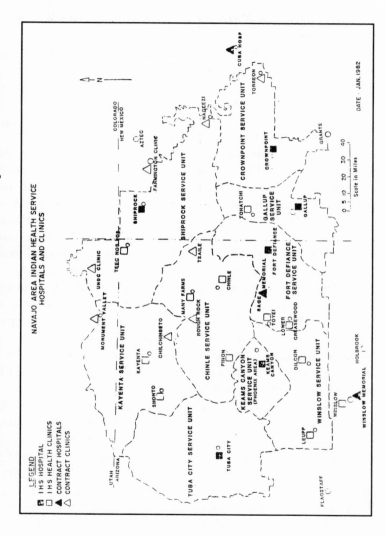

Source: Indian Health Service

Navajo Area Office in Window Rock, Arizona, serves "big Navajo" and Albuquerque Area Office serves the Alamo, Ramah, and Cañoncito bands. Navajos residing outside the service boundaries of other IHS Area Offices are not eligible for IHS services.

However, by focusing on "big Navajo," we capture data on the largest, most easily defined, culturally identical group of Indians anywhere in the United States. This group is served entirely by the NAIHS.

This report will concern itself with the Navajo, using other groups for comparison purposes. In interpreting time trend data, the all Indian comparison group presents yet another problem. The Indian Health Service usually reports data for "reservation states," states that have at least one federally recognized Indian reservation or "traditional Indian lands." Since 1972, Louisiana, Maine, New York, Pennsylvania, Connecticut, Rhode Island, Texas, Alabama, and Massachusetts have been added to the list in various years. There were, as of October 1, 1988, 33 "reservation states."

The Census Bureau suggests that the most accurate enumerations of American Indians are in "reservation states" (Passel, 1986), but Snipp (1989) argues that a nonmetropolitan bias is introduced by using only these states. However, Snipp is misinformed about which states are and are not "reservation states." For example, he states that California and Colorado are not considered Indian states, yet they are.

Of the estimated total American Indian population in 1985 (1,584,617), only eight percent (133,549) lived outside "reservation states." This suggests that use of IHS "reservation state" statistics will not introduce bias, other than that previously mentioned. For the all Indian comparison group in this report, I have chosen to use the data from tape only when comparable information is not available from IHS publications. The source for data in all tables and figures will be clearly labelled. Information presented from Snipp's book will refer to all enumerated persons who reported their race as Indian in the 1980 Census, and will be so noted. American Indians of mixed race may or may not report their race as Indian to the Census Bureau. On occasion, Snipp excludes Alaskan Natives from his statistics.

Figures 5–8 show population pyramids for all Indians and Navajos, 1985, and for the total U.S. population in 1980 and in 1940. The National Center for Health Statistics age-adjusted rates are all standardized to the 1940 U.S. population, as are the age-adjusted rates presented for Navajos and all Indians in this report.

Tables 2 through 5 detail the denominators used for most age-specific rate calculations for males and females. Occasionally, age groups have been collapsed, or previously published data for all Indians have been used.

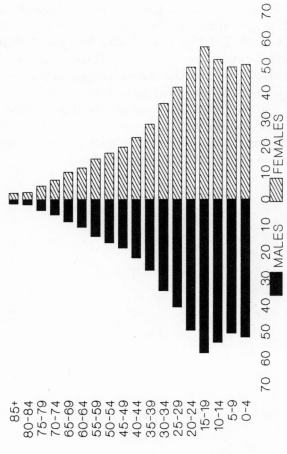

FIGURE 5
Population Pyramid
All Indians, 1985

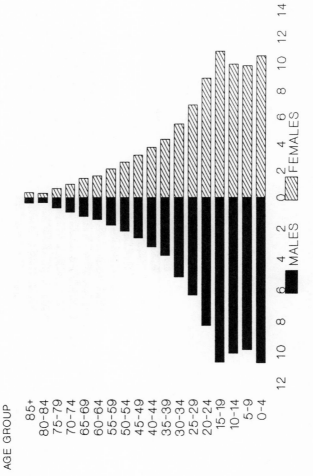

FIGURE 6
Population Pyramid
Navajos, 1985

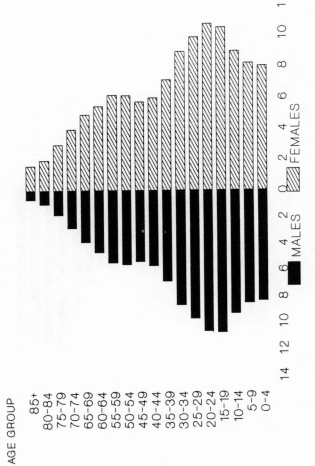

FIGURE 7
Population Pyramid
United States, 1980

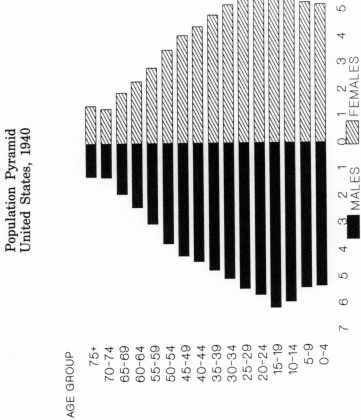

FIGURE 8
Population Pyramid
United States, 1940

AGE GROUP

75+
70-74
65-69
60-64
55-59
50-54
45-49
40-44
35-39
30-34
25-29
20-24
15-19
10-14
5-9
0-4

7 6 5 4 3 2 1 0 1 2 3 4 5 6 7

MALES   FEMALES

POPULATION IN MILLIONS

TABLE 2

Total American Indian 1985 Population Estimates* by
Detailed Age Group and Sex

Age Group	Male	Female	Total
<5	51,933	50,440	102,373
5–9	50,516	49,528	100,044
10–14	53,919	52,379	106,298
15–19	57,968	57,037	115,005
20–24	49,290	49,585	98,875
25–29	40,499	42,057	82,556
30–34	34,345	36,055	70,400
35–39	26,850	28,305	55,155
40–44	22,017	23,462	45,479
45–49	18,329	19,917	38,246
50–54	16,367	17,612	33,979
55–59	14,067	15,511	29,578
60–64	10,611	11,924	22,535
65–69	8,620	10,322	18,942
70–74	5,912	7,347	13,259
75–79	4,097	5,056	9,153
80–84	1,920	2,747	4,667
85+	1,559	2,357	3,916
Total	468,819	481,641	950,460

*Source: IHS

TABLE 3

Navajo 1985 Population Estimates*
by Detailed Age Group and Sex

Age Group	Male	Female	Total
<1	2,223	2,144	5,347
1–4	8,424	8,478	15,924
5–9	9,799	9,883	19,683
10–14	10,016	9,993	20,010
15–19	10,583	10,974	21,558
20–24	8,003	8,946	16,948
25–29	6,320	6,921	13,240
30–34	5,150	5,480	10,630
35–39	3,755	4,347	8,101
40–44	3,204	3,757	6,960
45–49	2,600	3,194	5,793
50–54	2,193	2,643	4,834
55–59	1,789	2,131	3,920
60–64	1,444	1,649	3,093
65–69	1,248	1,466	2,714
70–74	957	1,066	1,964
75–79	693	701	1,395
80–84	330	316	646
85+	344	390	734
Total	79,075	84,419	163,494

*Source: Adapted from NAIHS

TABLE 4

1985 Navajo Area Population Estimates*
by Collapsed Age Group and Sex

Age Group	Male	Female	Total
0–4	11,592	11,373	22,964
5–9	13 138	13 306	26,444
10–14	12,220	12,677	24,897
15–19	9,647	10,274	19,911
20–24	5,962	6,894	12,856
25–34	8,442	9,920	18,362
35–44	6,495	7,811	14,306
45–64	8,057	8,789	16,846
65+	3,522	3,386	6,908
Total	79,075	84,419	163,494

*Source: Adapted from NAIHS

TABLE 5

Midyear Population Estimates*, 1983–1986, Navajo Area,
by Service Unit

Service Unit	Year			
	1983	1984	1985	1986
Chinle	22,087	22,668	23,258	24,180
Crownpoint	12,175	12,470	12,768	13,204
Ft. Defiance	22,220	22,807	23,402	24,351
Gallup	23,313	23,904	25,504	25,551
Kayenta	12,896	13,215	13,538	14,062
Shiprock	34,263	35,106	35,964	37,384
Tuba City	18,607	19,137	19,676	20,407
Winslow	11,341	11,636	11,934	12,347
Total	157,902	160,943	166,044	171,486

*Source: NAIHS

Chapter **4**

FERTILITY

In this chapter, levels and patterns of fertility among the Navajo will be presented, as well as characteristics of the mother and outcomes of birth, especially patterns of prenatal care and low birth weight childbearing. Where possible, data are compared to other groups or earlier time periods.

Crude Birth Rates and General Fertility Rates

The Navajo birth rate, 33 births per 1000 population, is almost double the rate for the U.S. (Figure 9), and much higher even than the rate for blacks. The Navajo birth rate is comparable to 1985 rates for India, Mexico, and Venezuela (Kammeyer & Ginn, 1986). The crude birth rate for all Indians is 28 per 1000 population, higher than the U.S. black rate, but lower than the rate for Navajos.

The Navajo birth rate has fallen since 1965 when it was 55 per 1000 population, but it appears to have remained steady since the mid-1970s (Figure 10). In contrast, the U.S. total rate has dropped from only 19.4 to 15.8 per thousand population (NCHS, 1985). Earlier information about Navajo fertility is based on Morgan's (1973) study of the Ramah Navajo. Rates from 1890 to 1924 ranged from a high of 75.2 in the 1890–1894 period to a low of 41.1 in the 1925–1929 period, with a great deal of variation in between. There was no steady pattern of decline in the Morgan study years.

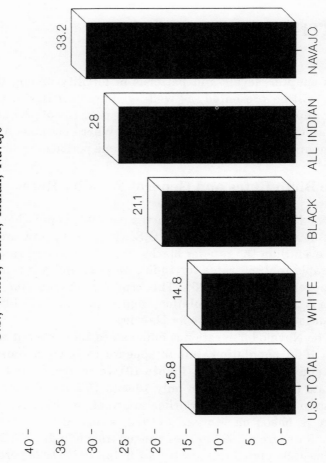

FIGURE 9

Crude Birth Rates*, 1985
U.S., White, Black, Indian, Navajo

*PER 1000 POPULATION

Source for Non-Indian Data: NCHS

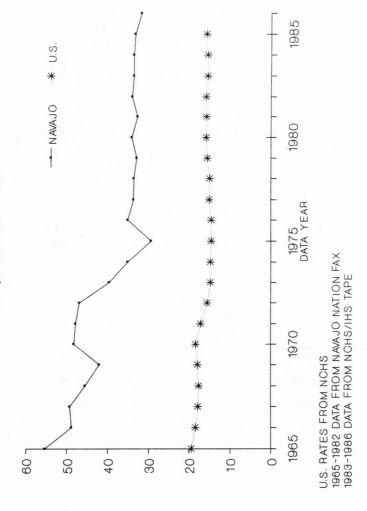

FIGURE 10

Crude Birth Rates Since 1965
Navajo and U.S. Total

NAVAJO   ✳ U.S.

U.S. RATES FROM NCHS
1965-1982 DATA FROM NAVAJO NATION FAX
1983-1986 DATA FROM NCHS/IHS TAPE

Subtracting the crude death rate from the crude birth rate yields the rate of natural increase (Figure 11). The Navajo population is increasing four times faster than the general U.S. population and more than twice as fast as the African American population. The rate of natural increase is as high, or higher, now than it was in the first part of the century for the Ramah Navajo (Morgan, 1973).

Comparisons of crude birth rates among groups can be misleading because of differences in age and sex structures within groups. Another more sensitive measure of period fertility is the general fertility rate: the number of births per thousand women aged 15–44. Using this measure, Navajo women are still bearing children at twice the U.S. rate (Figure 12). Tables 6 and 7 show the crude and general fertility rates by service unit by year. Crownpoint, Gallup, and Tuba City had the highest fertility rates on average, and Winslow the lowest. Tuba City also had the highest fertility in a study done by Kunitz (1983) in the early 1970s. This area is economically less developed than other parts of the reservation.

TABLE 6

Crude Birth Rates/1000 Population
1983–1986 Navajo Area, by Service Unit

Service Unit	Average All Yrs	1983	1984	1985	1986
Chinle	33.9	34.2	34.1	34.3	33.1
Crownpoint	36.3	37.4	35.6	36.4	35.0
Ft. Defiance	30.2	30.9	30.9	30.8	28.5
Gallup	36.5	36.4	37.9	34.7	36.0
Kayenta	31.8	32.9	31.6	31.1	31.4
Shiprock	32.8	33.6	33.8	33.0	30.5
Tuba City	36.4	38.4	34.3	38.4	34.6
Winslow	24.8	23.9	27.8	24.1	23.2
Total	33.2	33.6	33.6	33.3	31.8

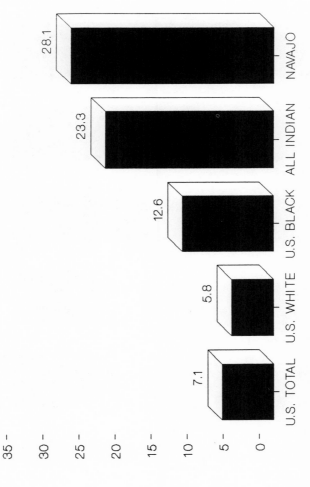

FIGURE 11
Rates* of Natural Increase**, 1985
U.S., White, Black, Indian, Navajo

35 –

30 –

25 –

20 –

15 –

10 –

5 –

0 –

7.1   5.8   12.6   23.3   28.1

U.S. TOTAL   U.S. WHITE   U.S. BLACK   ALL INDIAN   NAVAJO

*PER 1000 POPULATION PER YEAR
**CBR MINUS CDR

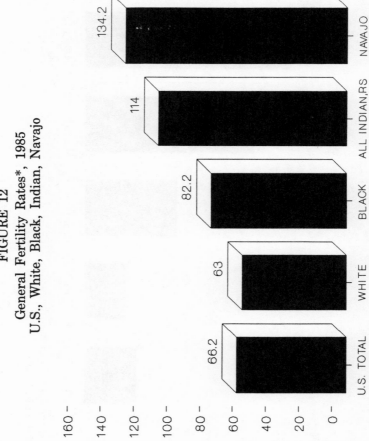

FIGURE 12
General Fertility Rates*, 1985
U.S., White, Black, Indian, Navajo

160 –

140 –

120 –

100 –

80 –

60 –

40 –

20 –

0 –

66.2 U.S. TOTAL

63 WHITE

82.2 BLACK

114 ALL INDIAN,RS

134.2 NAVAJO

*PER 1000 WOMEN AGE 15-44

TABLE 7
General Fertility Rates/1000 Women 15–44, 1983–1986
Navajo Area by Service Unit

Service Unit	Average All Yrs	1983	1984	1985	1986
Chinle	158.3	159.7	159.1	160.1	154.5
Crownpoint	169.2	174.3	166.1	169.9	163.2
Ft. Defiance	141.0	144.2	144.0	143.9	133.0
Gallup	170.3	169.7	176.8	161.7	167.8
Kayenta	148.1	153.4	147.2	145.1	146.3
Shiprock	152.9	156.6	157.7	155.0	142.4
Tuba City	169.8	179.3	159.9	179.3	161.2
Winslow	115.8	111.5	129.9	112.6	108.1
Total	154.8	156.8	156.8	155.4	148.2

Age Specific and Total Fertility Rates

For U.S. whites, age specific fertility rates peak in the 25–29 age group, but for blacks and Navajos the rates peak in the 20–24 age group (Figure 13). After that age, black rates converge with age specific rates for whites. The entire excess of African American fertility compared to white can be accounted for in childbearing before age 25. For Navajos, however, childbearing begins early, and the age specific rates do not converge with whites until the oldest age group (45–49).

These age specific rates summed produce a total fertility rate in Navajos of two children per woman more than average white fertility (Figure 14). Black total fertility is only slightly higher (2.2 children per woman) than the 1.8 for U.S. total. Black fertility begins early and ends early, but Navajo fertility begins early and continues.

Broudy and May (1983) found a dramatic decline in the Navajo crude birth rate from 55.4 in 1964 to 33.1 in 1978. However, if we are looking for evidence of further fertility decline among the Navajo, neither the age-specific fertility

FIGURE 13
Age-Specific Fertility Rates, 1985*
U.S., White, Black, Indian, Navajo

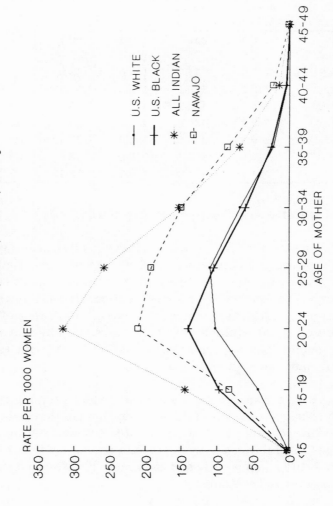

INDIAN RATES 1983-86 AVERAGE

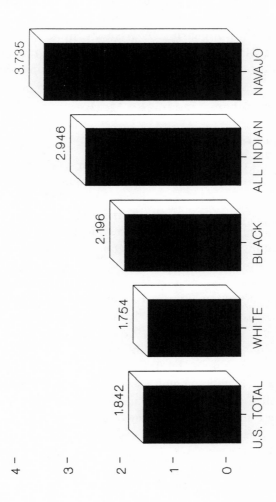

FIGURE 14

Total Fertility Rates*, 1985
U.S., White, Black, Indian, Navajo

5 –
4 –
3 –
2 –
1 –
0 –

1.842 — U.S. TOTAL
1.754 — WHITE
2.196 — BLACK
2.946 — ALL INDIAN
3.735 — NAVAJO

*PER WOMAN; ALL INDIAN RATE 1986

rates, nor total fertility rates provides it. Rates are elevated in all but the youngest age group. It is possible that, over time, Navajo childbearing will be concentrated in the younger age groups, but end earlier, like the pattern found in blacks. There is little to suggest that fertility will be curtailed by delayed childbearing. A greater emphasis on post-secondary education for women may hold the greatest promise for eventual reduction in the early childbearing pattern.

Characteristics of the Mother

Prenatal Care

Prenatal care began in the first trimester for almost half the live births. Of the Navajo women giving birth between 1983 and 1986, 29% began prenatal care in the second trimester, 13% in the third trimester, and five percent received no prenatal care. In 1990, 24% of New Mexico Navajo women received little or no prenatal care (New Mexico Department of Health, 1992).

Despite the fact that free prenatal care is available to Navajo women, Figure 15 shows lower utilization of prenatal care than African Americans and Hispanics. By the fourth month of pregnancy, 40% of Navajo women had still not sought prenatal care. While 60% of U.S. white women begin prenatal care in the first or second month of pregnancy, only 37% of Navajo women do so. Between one third and one half of all the minority comparison women wait until at least the fourth month of pregnancy to seek care.

Figure 16 shows changes in Navajo prenatal care patterns over time. A study of prenatal care patterns in the 1950s by Loughlin (cited in Kunitz, 1983) found that only about 10% of pregnant women sought prenatal care in the first trimester in the 1955–1960 time period, while nearly half sought no prenatal care at all during pregnancy. Slocumb and Kunitz (1977) found a large reduction in the proportion of women who received no prenatal care in the time period

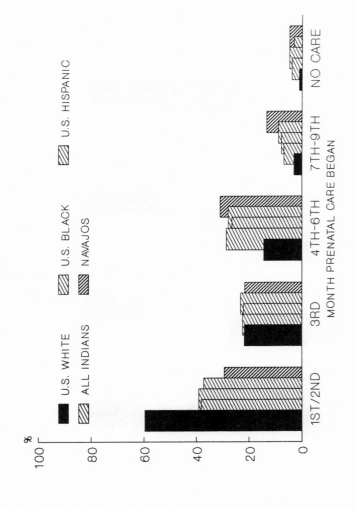

FIGURE 15
Prenatal Care Patterns
U.S. White, Black, Hispanic, Indian

Source Non-Indian Data: NCHS

FIGURE 16
Navajo Prenatal Care Patterns in Three Time Periods

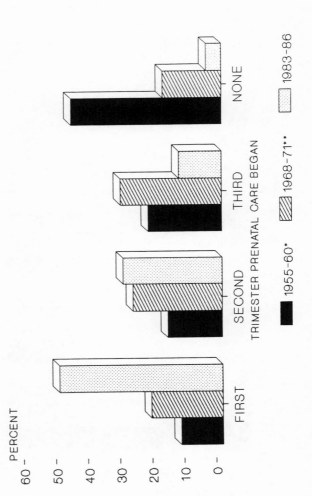

*Source: Loughlin (in Kunitz, 1983)
**Source: Slocumb & Kunitz, 1977

1968–1971. While the current prenatal care patterns are less than optimal, it is apparent that significant progress has been achieved in delivering prenatal care to this population. The most recent data from New Mexico indicate that this trend is continuing (New Mexico Department of Health, 1992).

Married women were somewhat more likely than unmarried women to begin prenatal care in the first trimester (Table 8), as were women with more education (Table 9). A steady increase in the proportion of women obtaining early prenatal care and a decline in those receiving no prenatal care can be observed as the level of education increases.

There is a relationship between prenatal care and birth outcome. A larger proportion of Navajo women giving birth to low birthweight babies received no prenatal care (11.4%), compared to women who delivered babies weighing at least 2500 grams (4.1%) (Table 10). A larger proportion of women whose prenatal care status was unknown were also in the low birth weight category, 9.7% compared to 4.5% delivering normal weight infants. Low birth weight outcomes will be discussed in greater detail later in this chapter.

TABLE 8

Prenatal Care by Marital Status of Mother*
Navajo Area Births, 1983–1986

Prenatal Care Started in:	Marital Status	
	Married (N = 11,053)	Unmarried (N = 10,636)
First Trimester	53.9%	42.9%
Second Trimester	27.8%	31.1%
Third Trimester	10.4%	15.1%
No Prenatal Care	3.1%	6.1%
Unknown	4.8%	4.8%

*Marital status not stated in 6 cases

TABLE 9

Prenatal Care by Mother's Education
Navajo Area Births, 1983–1986

Trimester Prenatal Care Started	Mother's Education in Years					
	<8	9–11	12	>12	Unk	Total
First	39.3%	43.2%	50.8%	59.0%	40.0%	48.5%
Second	31.0%	30.3%	29.8%	26.2%	29.3%	29.4%
Third	16.4%	15.8%	11.4%	7.9%	14.1%	12.7%
No Care	8.2%	5.9%	3.5%	2.1%	6.9%	4.5%
Unknown	5.0%	4.8%	4.5%	4.7%	9.7%	4.8%

TABLE 10

Prenatal Care and Low Birth Weight*
Navajo Area Births 1983–1986

Trimester Prenatal Care Started	Birth Weight	
	< 2500 Grams (N = 1,210)	> = 2500 Grams (N = 20,434)
First	40.4%	49.0%
Second	25.7%	29.6%
Third	12.8%	12.7%
No Care	11.4%	4.1%
Unknown	9.7%	4.5%

*Birth Weight not stated in 51 cases

Age at First Birth

The median age of Navajo mothers giving birth in this time period was 22 years, the range extending from a low of 12 to a high of 43. This is two years younger than the median age of the all Indian and U.S. black comparison groups, and four years younger than U.S. whites (Figure 17). Forty-three

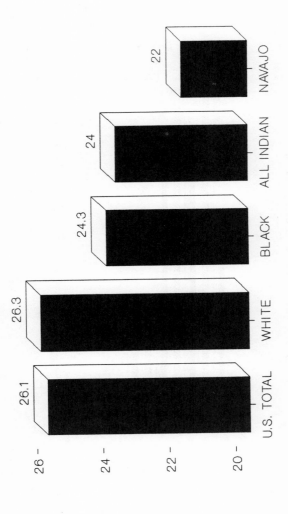

FIGURE 17

Median Age of Childbearing, 1985
U.S., White, Black, Indian, Navajo

Source Non-Indian Data: NCHS

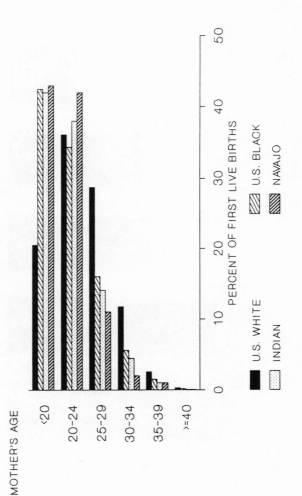

FIGURE 18
Age at Birth of First Child
U.S. White, Black, Indian, Navajo

MOTHER'S AGE

<20

20-24

25-29

30-34

35-39

>=40

0   10   20   30   40   50

PERCENT OF FIRST LIVE BIRTHS

U.S. WHITE   U.S. BLACK

INDIAN   NAVAJO

U.S. 1985, All Indian 84–86
Source Non-Indian Data: NCHS

percent of Navajo first births were to women under 20 years of age, exactly the same proportion as in U.S. blacks. For U.S. whites, 20% were to teen mothers (Figure 18). Less than 5% of Navajo first births were to women past the age of thirty; 15% of U.S. white births were to women over 30. The Navajo and all Indian pattern of first births were very similar, with a tendency toward even younger childbearing in the Navajo. Of all Navajo births, 17.1% were to teens. In 1990, the percent of New Mexico Navajo births to teen mothers was 15.6% (New Mexico Department of Health, 1992).

Geronimus (1987) suggests that teen motherhood in industrialized societies is a social response to disadvantage. She notes that almost all the teen childbearing in the United States occurs among disadvantaged groups, among those with the fewest opportunities for extended adolescence (e.g., college). This author asks us to look at the social reality of those young women who bear children early, and to realize that the term "adolescence" is not only of relatively recent origin, but varies across cultures. The supposed biological and social immaturity of these women may be overshadowed by a number of risk factors that accumulate over time and negatively impact on the health status of their offspring. These factors include poor nutrition, sexually transmitted disease, inadequate housing, education, and employment opportunities. It may be that having children at a young age is advantageous for this group.

Births to Single Women

Almost half the Navajo births were to unmarried mothers. This rate of single childbearing is more than three times higher than in the white population, and approaches the rate in the black population (Figure 19). The rate for all Indians is also high, 40%. In 1987, one fourth of all U.S. births, 17% of white and 62% of black births were to unmarried mothers (Bianchi, 1990). Single childbearing has

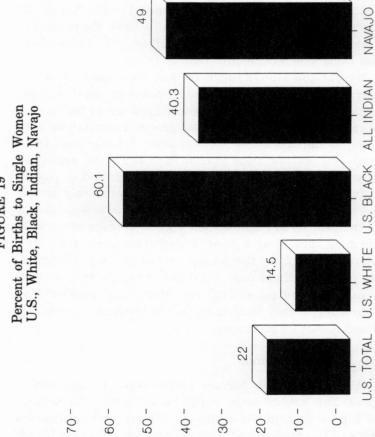

FIGURE 19
Percent of Births to Single Women
U.S., White, Black, Indian, Navajo

Source Non-Indian Data: NCHS

increased dramatically since 1960 when the rates were 2.3% for whites and 22% for blacks (Bianchi, 1990).

Since this study was completed, Navajo single childbearing has apparently increased. Of New Mexico Navajo births in 1990, 60.4% were born to single women (New Mexico Department of Health, 1992).

For all groups, the rate of single childbearing is highest for first births (Figure 20). The patterns then diverge: for whites there is a slight increase in single childbearing at the higher birth orders; U.S. blacks and all Indians level off after the initial decline; and rates for Navajos continue to decline with increasing birth order.

Figure 21 shows the percentage of births to single mothers by service unit. Kayenta and Winslow areas had the lowest rates (43% and 44%, respectively), and Gallup had the highest (56%). The service units with the lowest general fertility rates had the lowest rates of single childbearing, and vice versa.

The frequency of female-headed families has been increasing, not only in this country, but worldwide in the last few decades (Lancaster, 1989). In the past, this type of family resulted mainly from death or abandonment of the spouse. But the current rise results from new pathways, predictable from evolutionary theory (Lancaster, 1989). Lancaster discusses three conditions that are becoming more prevalent worldwide and predispose to the formation of single-parent families headed by women.

If resources sufficient to raise children are available to women, then the role of the male as provisioner becomes redundant. Women may marry late or not at all, may divorce, or not remarry after the death of a spouse. In some tribal and horticultural societies, polygyny is associated with the woman being the primary economic provider. Women view polygyny as advantageous because the cost of providing for the husband is shared, and men can afford more than one wife because

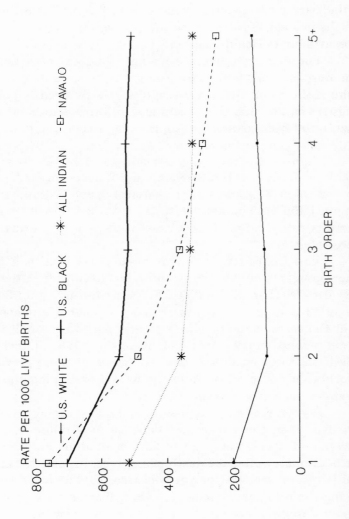

FIGURE 20

Births to Single Women by Birth Order
U.S. White, Black, Indian, Navajo

Source Non-Indian Data: NCHS

FIGURE 21

Percent of Navajo Births to Single Women by Service Unit

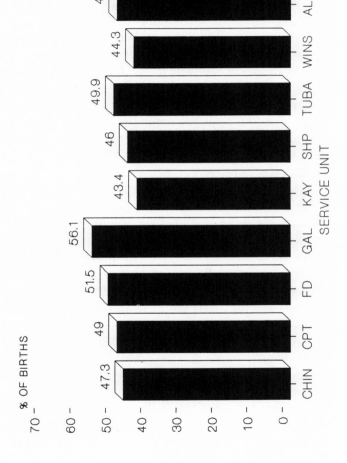

they do not have to consider the cost of providing for her and her children.

A second predisposing condition results when men and women have insufficient or unpredictable access to resources for provisioning. Under these conditions, women attempt to maximize their reproductive success by excluding men from the household, and by forming maternal kin networks or by forming liaisons with more than one man and his kin, simultaneously or serially, thus broadening the resource base from which they and their children can benefit. This situation has been most prevalent in the United States and in modern state societies with large groups of undereducated, chronically unemployed males. Under these conditions the sex ratios of eligible men to women during the reproductive years becomes unbalanced, as a result of higher rates of incarceration, drug and alcohol addiction, and higher mortality from risk taking and violent behaviors.

The Third World complement to this scenario is the impelled rural to urban and international migration of males to compete in an increasingly non-agricultural labor market. Women are left, temporarily or permanently, in rural areas with the children, and men may or may not send remittances to them. If remittances are sent, they are used, not for investment or capital formation, but to provide basic necessities for the family, thus fueling a repetition of the cycle.

As Lancaster (1989) points out, it should not be surprising that the single-parent, female-headed household is becoming a dominant family pattern worldwide. In the case of the Navajo, perhaps all three of the above scenarios exist to some degree, combined with a preexisting matrifocal family orientation, predisposing this group to very high rates of single childbearing. Selected census data on the Navajo Reservation area suggest that almost a third of children under 18 years old live with only one parent (Navajo Nation, 1988) and that 24% of families are headed by women with no husband present. It is not possible from these data to ascertain the extent of spousal involvement in child rearing and provisioning for those women who are married.

Birth Order

As mentioned earlier, Navajo childbearing begins early and continues longer than childbearing in other groups. Fifteen percent of all Navajo births were fifth and higher order children, compared to the U.S. where only 3.8% of births were fifth and higher order (Table 11). Even in the 15–19 age group of the mother, one fourth of Navajo births were second or higher order. In the 20–24 age group, first births accounted for only 37% of births. Over half the births to U.S. whites in this age group were first births, as were 40% of U.S. black births.

Women with at least a high school education were proportionately less likely to have five or more children, although equally as likely as the other education groups to have four (Table 12). Twice the proportion of the women in the less than eight years of education category were having fifth or higher order births, compared to women in the next highest education category, 9 to 11 years.

Navajo fathers were, on average, two years older than mothers for birth orders one through three. At older birth orders, they were three years older than mothers. However, the percent of fathers with age not recorded was 51% for first births. Thereafter, the percent steadily declined, but even at birth orders of five and above, 16% of fathers' ages were not recorded on the birth certificates. Because data were missing on so many of the fathers, more detailed analyses of the father's characteristics were not performed.

TABLE 11

Age of Mother by Birth Order
Navajo Area Births, 1983–1986

Age Group	Total Live Births	Birth Order					
		1	2	3	4	>5	UNK
		(Percent Distribution)					
<15	67	95.5	3.0	—	—	—	1.5
15–19	3,643	75.1	20.7	3.5	0.4	0.1	0.1
20–24	7,528	36.5	35.9	18.8	6.6	2.0	0.2
25–29	5,321	13.9	25.4	27.4	17.9	15.3	0.1
30–34	3,289	5.5	13.9	23.7	23.4	34.4	0.1
35–39	1,491	3.1	6.3	14.5	20.5	55.5	—
40–44	337	2.4	6.2	7.1	9.5	74.8	—
45–49	19	—	—	5.3	—	94.7	—
Total	21,695	30.1	24.8	18.5	11.7	14.7	.1

TABLE 12

Education of Mother by Birth Order
Navajo Area Births, 1983–1986

Mother's Education (Years)	Total Live Births	Birth Order					
		1	2	3	4	5	UNK
		(Percent Distribution)					
<8	1,848	18.2	16.5	16.3	12.5	36.5	—
9–11	6,921	30.4	22.6	18.1	12.0	16.8	0.1
12	8,404	32.1	27.4	19.0	11.0	10.4	0.1
>12	3,850	31.0	27.8	19.6	12.1	9.5	0.1
Not Stated	672	29.3	20.5	17.4	12.2	18.8	1.8

Interbirth Intervals

Approximately 20% of Navajo second and higher order births preceded by a live birth were spaced less than 18 months apart (Table 13). At the other extreme, over one-fourth were spaced at intervals longer than four years. Detailed information on interbirth interval is not presented for births preceded by a termination because pregnancy terminations are not separated into voluntary and involuntary in the coding scheme. However, 38% of births to women with a termination immediately prior were born four or more years after the previous pregnancy.

Table 14 compares the mean interbirth intervals for Navajos and U.S. whites and blacks. At the lower birth orders, Navajo women have the shortest mean interval and U.S. blacks have the longest. At birth orders above four, U.S. whites have the longest mean interval. Higher birth orders are associated with shorter interbirth intervals, as would be expected.

TABLE 13

Birth Order by Interbirth Interval
Second and Higher Order Singleton Births
Preceded by a Live Birth
Navajo Births 1983–1986

Birth Order	Interbirth Interval (Months)					
	1–11	12–17	18–23	24–35	36–47	48+
Second	2.5	17.3	17.6	22.9	12.8	26.8
Third	1.9	16.2	15.2	23.2	12.6	30.8
Fourth	1.8	17.3	15.4	20.9	12.9	31.7
Fifth & Higher	2.7	18.5	16.7	24.6	13.9	23.5
Total*	2.3	17.2	16.4	23.0	13.0	28.1

*Excluding births for which interbirth interval was unknown.

TABLE 14
Mean Interval (Months) Since Last Live Birth by Birth Order
Navajo, 1983–86, U.S. White and Black, 1985

Birth Order	Navajo	U.S. White	U.S. Black
First & Second	41.9	43.7	52.4
Second & Third	44.3	46.8	49.0
Third & Fourth	43.3	44.6	44.6
Fourth & Fifth	41.5	43.3	41.9
Fifth & Sixth	40.6	41.8	40.0
Sixth & Seventh	39.2	40.1	38.6
Eighth & Higher	35.5	36.3	35.5

Hospital Births Attended by a Physician

Virtually all (99.6%) births in the Navajo area occurred in a hospital, which is surprising considering the geography of the area. This is a departure from earlier years when there were fewer hospital, physician-attended births. Broudy and May (1983) identified this trend toward hospital deliveries in 1978 data when over 85% of births occurred in a hospital. They report that only 61% of births were hospital deliveries in 1965. Hospital deliveries accounted for 99.0% of all U.S. births in 1985, 98.9% for whites, and 99.3% for the other than white category (NCHS, 1985). The slightly lower rate for whites probably reflects the recent trend toward home and birthing clinic births attended by midwives, not present in the Navajo.

Utilizing 1980 census data, the Navajo Nation's Statistical Abstract reports that 60% of residents required more than thirty minutes to reach a health care facility, and 32% required more than an hour to reach a facility (Navajo Nation, 1988). Moreover, one-fourth of the households had no vehicle available to them and three-fourths of the roads on the reservation were unpaved (Navajo Nation, 1988). Thus, the seemingly insurmountable obstacles of remoteness of residence and distance to a hospital have apparently been overcome.

Birth Outcomes

In this section, information regarding sex ratios at birth, birth weight of infants, and Apgar scores of newborns will be presented.

Secondary Sex Ratios

The secondary sex ratio is the ratio of males to females at birth. The primary sex ratio refers to the ratio at conception, and is not generally known, except that research on fetal deaths indicates that many more males than females die in utero. In the United States, the sex ratio at birth is approximately 106 males per 100 white females, 103 for blacks, and 105 total. The sex ratio for Navajos is 103.2 (Figure 22). The Navajo sex ratio of live births fell from 1983, when it was 106, to 99 in 1986. In 1984 and 1985 it was 104.

The sex ratio is highest for mothers under age 25 and over age 35. Figure 23 shows the sex ratio by age and marital status. Overall, sex ratios are higher for unmarried (104.1) than for married (100.9) mothers. This surprising finding contradicts what Guttentag and Secord (1983) refer to as a "long known fact" that sex ratios at birth are lower for illegitimate births, irrespective of race or geography (p. 210). They postulate that more illegitimate than legitimate pregnancies are unwanted, and that access and incentive for prenatal care would be less in the unmarried group of women, disproportionately affecting males. While it is a plausible explanation in support of their thesis, our data do not support the thesis itself. A more recent article by Chahnazarian (1988) states that the sex ratio is unaffected by legitimacy.

Guttentag and Secord (1983) posit another, more tentative link between male promiscuity, infrequent female intercourse, and lower sex ratios at birth. They cite evidence from James (1984) that sex ratios in monogamous tribes are well above 100, and well below 100 in polygynous tribes.

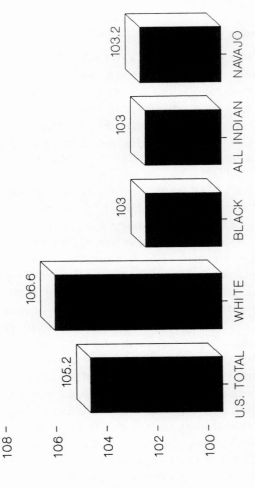

FIGURE 22
Sex Ratios at Birth, 1985
U.S., White, Black, Indian, Navajo

MALES/FEMALES × 100

Source Non-Indian Data: NCHS

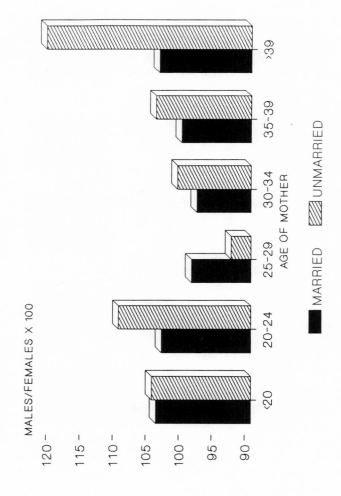

FIGURE 23

Navajo Sex Ratios at Birth by Mother's Age and Marital Status

These observations rest on the biological argument that a higher coital rate for females affects the timing of intercourse so that it more often coincides with ovulation, and thus favors male conceptions.

Figure 24 shows Navajo sex ratios by birth order. They are lowest for birth orders of five and above, and highest for first births. These observations fit well with data from almost every other study investigating sex ratios. Chahnazarian (1988) provides a literature review of the determinants of the sex ratio at birth. In every study that included birth order, the effects of increasing birth order were either negative or, occasionally, nil.

This relationship also fits with the reasoning that higher coital frequency results in more male births, if we assume that women becoming pregnant for the first time are more sexually active than older women. This is probably a reasonable assumption for married women. It does not, however, explain the high sex ratio of Navajo first births, given that so many of the mothers are unmarried teens who presumably are in less stable pair bonds. Can we assume their coital frequency is the same as slightly older married women?

Figure 25 shows the sex ratio at birth by month of birth. Sex ratios are highest for spring births (April, May and June), well above 105:100. They are lowest for fall births (September through December), well below unity. Chahnazarian's (1988) review of the determinants of sex ratio at birth in the recent literature makes no mention of seasonal variation, and I am at a loss to explain the tremendous variation we see in the Navajo data. It is possibly worth further investigation. Another possible explanation for deviant sex ratios has been explored by Hesser, Blumberg and Drew (1975). They found significantly altered sex ratios resulting from parents who tested positive for a hepatitis B surface antigen in a Greek population. They also cite earlier studies of three Melanesian

FIGURE 24
Navajo Sex Ratios at Birth by Birth Order

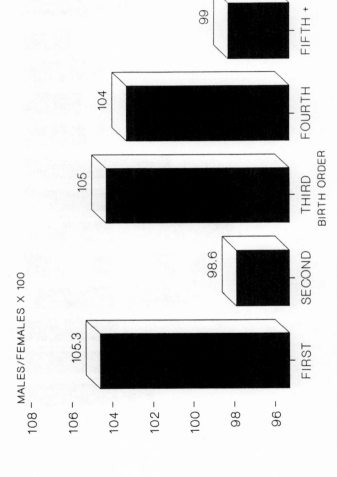

MALES/FEMALES X 100

*FIFTH OR HIGHER BIRTH ORDER

FIGURE 25

Navajo Sex Ratios at Birth by Month of Birth

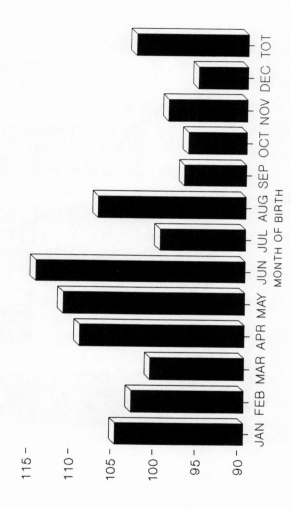

populations with altered sex ratios of offspring of parents with the antigen. This antigen is associated with viral hepatitis and some other diseases. The prevalence of HBsAg carriers ranges from less than one percent in the U.S. population to over 20 percent in some Pacific Islander populations (Hesser, et al., 1975). I am not aware of any studies of the prevalence of this antigen in the Navajo or other Amerindian population groups, but it is an area which may merit further exploration. As the authors of this article point out, if one infectious agent can produce sex differences in offspring, then it is not unlikely that other infectious agents may also produce effects.

Other researchers have focused on the low sex ratio of the Navajo, linking it to the possible mutagenic effects of radiation exposure generated by uranium mining activity in the area (Waxweiler & Roscoe, 1981; Archer, 1981). They studied only first births to control for birth order effects, and found that among uranium miners exposed to radiation (Navajo and other miners), fathers younger than 25 had fewer sons than fathers over 25. This result was the opposite of what they would have predicted, given that fathers over age 25 would presumably have had higher levels of exposure than younger fathers. Their results do coincide, however, with seven of nine studies reviewed by Chahnazarian (1988), reporting that younger fathers have more male births. Among the unexposed Indian miners in the Waxweiler study, sex ratios were higher than among unexposed white miners. These findings are puzzling, and do not provide a ready explanation for the Navajo low sex ratio phenomenon. It is most likely that among the many variables which may influence the sex ratio at birth, low levels of radiation exposure are either not significant, or not significantly prevalent among Navajos to exert much effect.

Figure 26 shows the variation in sex ratio by service unit within the Navajo reservation. The areas with the lowest sex ratios are Winslow, Chinle, and Tuba City. The areas with sex ratios well above the tribe's average are Crownpoint, Fort

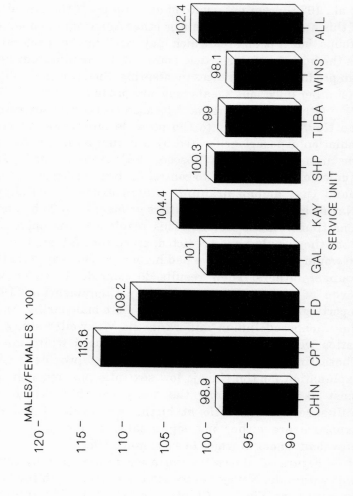

FIGURE 26

Navajo Sex Ratios at Birth by Service Unit

Defiance, and Kayenta. The service units with former uranium activity include Shiprock, Tuba City and Kayenta, one unit each from the high, medium and low sex ratio groups.

I believe that the most straightforward explanation for the low sex ratio of Navajo births lies in the increased susceptibility of males to death; under the relatively harsh conditions still present on the Navajo reservation and the less than optimal utilization of prenatal care, males might have higher gestational mortality compared to females.

Birth Weight

Navajo women are not at increased risk of bearing low birth weight babies (<2500 grams) compared to U.S. whites (Figure 27), despite the high prevalence of factors normally associated with low birth weight such as low education, poverty, early childbearing, high parity, and births to unmarried women. Where one would expect to find a profile of low birth weight childbearing similar to U.S. blacks, the profile of American Indians, particularly Navajos, more closely resembles the profile for U.S. whites. Of every 1000 live births, U.S. white women bear 56 that weigh less than 2500 grams; Navajo women bear only 52. This is in strong contrast to the U.S. black population where 124 of every 1000 live births weigh less than 2500 grams. The most recent data from New Mexico indicate that the Navajo pattern has changed only slightly: 59 infants were born weighing less than 2500 grams per 1000 births in 1990 (New Mexico Department of Health, 1992).

The median birth weight for Navajo babies is 3320 grams, around 7.2 pounds (Figure 28). This is only 100 grams less than the median birth weight of U.S. white newborns. U.S. black infants weighed the least, on average. Male Navajo infants weighed slightly more than females, as did second and higher order births compared to first births.

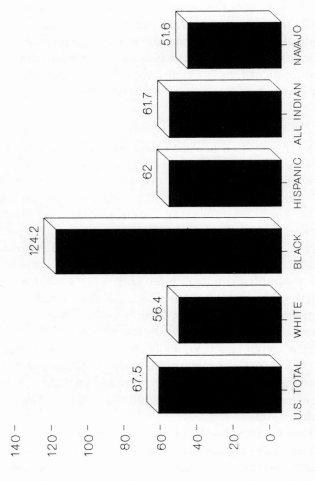

FIGURE 27
Rates* of Low Birth Weight**
U.S., White, Black, Hispanic, Indian

*PER 1000 LIVE BIRTHS; ** <2500 GRAMS

Source Non-Indian Data: NCHS

FIGURE 28
Median Birth Weight in Grams
U.S., White, Black, Indian, Navajo

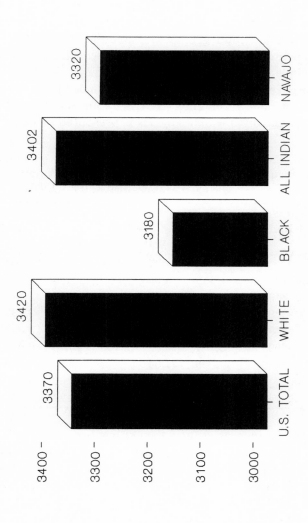

Source Non-Indian Data: NCHS

The incidence of very low birth weight (less than 1500 grams) was 7.5 per thousand Navajo live births, compared to 9.4 per thousand for U.S. whites and 26.9 for U.S. blacks in 1985 (NCHS, 1989). At the upper end of the birth weight scale, 9.3 Navajo infants per thousand live births weighed more than 4500 grams (9.9 pounds), indicating, perhaps, offspring of diabetic mothers. However, a smaller proportion of Navajo than white babies weighed over 3500 grams (34.3%, compared to 44%). Only 26% of black births weighed over 3500 grams, 7.7 pounds (NCHS, 1989). A detailed breakdown of Navajo birth weights by sex is presented in Table 15.

TABLE 15
Frequency and Percent Distribution of Weight (Grams)
Navajo Area Live Births, 1983–1986

Birth Weight (Grams)	Male		Female		Total	
	#	%	#	%	#	%
<1500	84	.77	79	.74	163	.75
1500–1999	120	1.09	116	1.08	236	1.09
2000–2499	384	3.50	427	3.98	811	3.74
2500–2999	1,666	15.18	2,071	19.32	3,737	17.23
3000–3499	4,473	40.75	4,621	43.11	9,094	41.92
3500–3999	3,259	29.69	2,763	25.78	6,022	27.76
4000–4499	839	7.64	540	5.04	1,379	6.36
>4500	129	1.17	73	.68	202	.93
Not Stated	22	.20	29	.27	51	.24

An increased incidence of low birth weight babies born to teen mothers was not observed in data for all Indians (Figure 29). For the age group under 15 in Navajos, the numbers were too small to draw a conclusion (one low birth weight baby in 66 live births). It appears that, for Indian women, the risk of bearing a low birth weight baby increases substantially only after age 39.

FIGURE 29
Low Birth Weight by Age of Mother
U.S. White, U.S. Black, All Indians, Navajo

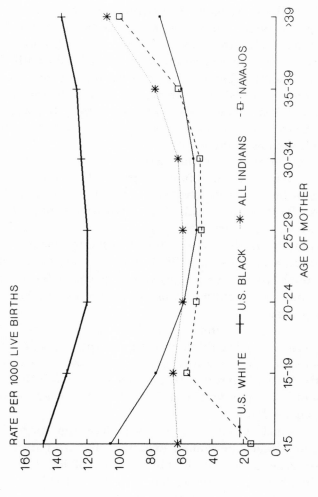

*LESS THAN 2500 GRAMS

Source Non-Indian Data: NCHS

For Indian and Navajo women, education decreases the incidence of low birth weight, as it does for blacks and for whites in the U.S. (Figure 30). However, Navajo women with less than eight years of education bear fewer low weight infants than African American women with a college education! Being unmarried does little to increase the risk of bearing a low birth infant in Indian women (Figure 31). The relative risk of unmarried to married is 1.3 for both Navajos and all Indians. The relative risk is greatest for U.S. whites (1.7) and intermediate for blacks (1.4). It appears from these data and from other studies (Johnson, 1987), that when single childbearing is the norm, the deleterious effects associated with it are not as great.

Incomplete gestation accounts for the vast majority of all low birth weight infants (Figure 32). Preterm incidence rates of low birth weight are highest for blacks (418.0) and lowest for Navajos (192.2). Low birth weight in gestations of 37 weeks or more are caused by intrauterine growth retardation which has been linked with nutrition and smoking (Kleinman & Kopstein, 1987). For full term births, rates of low birth weight are approximately equal for whites, all Indians, and Navajos, and they are double for African Americans.

Figure 33 shows the rate of low birth weight childbearing by interbirth interval. Navajos appear to be least affected by short birth intervals, and blacks most affected. Birth intervals beyond 12 months show a relatively stable rate of low birth weight childbearing. However, black rates are, again, double.

In fact, for almost every variable, except marital status, African American women exhibit the same pattern as the other groups, but at double the rate of low birth weight infants. Numerous studies have attributed the high incidence of low birth weight in blacks to the lingering effects of poverty, but in fact, the Navajo is just as impoverished, if not more so, than the black population.

FIGURE 30

Low Birth Weight* by Mother's Education
U.S. White, U.S. Black, Indian, Navajo

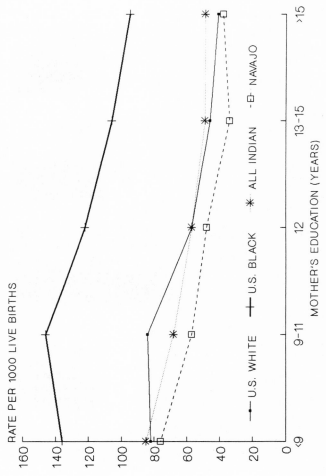

RATE PER 1000 LIVE BIRTHS

MOTHER'S EDUCATION (YEARS)

—●— U.S. WHITE   —+— U.S. BLACK   —✳— ALL INDIAN   -◻- NAVAJO

*LESS THAN 2500 GRAMS

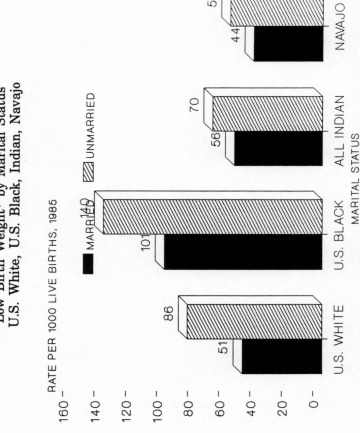

FIGURE 31
Low Birth Weight* by Marital Status
U.S. White, U.S. Black, Indian, Navajo

RATE PER 1000 LIVE BIRTHS, 1985

■ MARRIED ▨ UNMARRIED

160 –
140 –
120 –
100 –
80 –
60 –
40 –
20 –
0 –

U.S. WHITE   U.S. BLACK   ALL INDIAN   NAVAJO

MARITAL STATUS

U.S. WHITE: 51, 86
U.S. BLACK: 101, 140
ALL INDIAN: 56, 70
NAVAJO: 44, 59

*LESS THAN 2500 GRAMS

FIGURE 32
Low Birth Weight* by Gestation
U.S. White, U.S. Black, Indian, Navajo

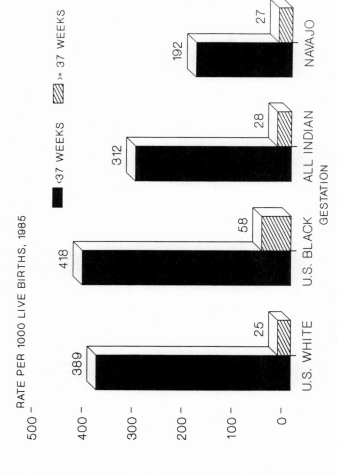

RATE PER 1000 LIVE BIRTHS, 1985

■ <37 WEEKS   ▨ >= 37 WEEKS

500 —

400 —

300 —

200 —

100 —

0 —

389   25   U.S. WHITE

418   58   U.S. BLACK

312   28   ALL INDIAN

192   27   NAVAJO

GESTATION

*LESS THAN 2500 GRAMS

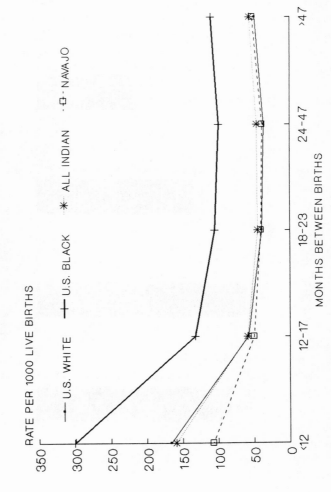

FIGURE 33
Low Birth Weight* by Interbirth Interval
U.S. White, U.S. Black, Indian, Navajo

RATE PER 1000 LIVE BIRTHS

—•— U.S. WHITE   —+— U.S. BLACK   —✳— ALL INDIAN   ·⊡· NAVAJO

MONTHS BETWEEN BIRTHS

*LESS THAN 2500 GRAMS
**SECOND AND HIGHER ORDER BIRTHS

The overarching question then, with regard to low birth weight, is why the Indian pattern is virtually identical to that of the privileged white group, and not at all similar to the African American whom they resemble in many socioeconomic and cultural ways. Possible explanations include biological, cultural, behavioral, and the differential availability of health care between the two groups, or some combination of these factors.

Congenital Malformations

As has been found in other studies (McCormick, 1985), Navajo low birth weight babies are about twice as likely to have congenital malformations as are babies of normal weight. Five percent of low birth weight Navajo infants had congenital malformations recorded on the birth certificate, compared to 2.4% of normal weight infants. Congenital malformations were recorded on 2.6% of all Navajo births in this time period, almost three times the rate in the general U.S. population (New Mexico Health and Environment Department, 1989).

May, et al. (1983) found that fetal alcohol syndrome (FAS) was the principal cause of birth defects among southwestern Indians. A screening program identified 5.2/1000 Navajo children aged 0–4 as having either FAS or fetal alcohol effect (FAE) in 1982.

Since the birth and death certificates were not linked, comparisons of survival rates by birth weight or presence of congenital anomalies was not possible. However, more detailed information on fatal congenital anomalies can be found in Chapter 6, "Infant Mortality."

Apgar Scores

The Apgar score is a summary measure of the infant's condition at birth. It is appraised at both one and five minutes after birth. Five characteristics of the infant are evaluated on a scale of 0, 1 or 2. These clinical impressions are summed for the total score, which may range from zero to ten. The five signs include heart rate, respiratory effort, muscle tone, reflex irritability, and color. Scores of seven and above indicate that the infant is in satisfactory condition. Lower scores indicate progressively poorer condition.

Table 16 depicts the percent distribution of 1-minute Apgar scores for Navajo, U.S. white, and U.S. black. As can be seen, the overwhelming majority of births have Apgar scores in the satisfactory range (seven or above): 90.8% of both Navajos and U.S. whites, and 87.8% of U.S. blacks.

TABLE 16

Percent Distribution of One Minute Apgar Scores
Navajo 1983–1986, U.S. White and Black, 1985*

Apgar Score	Navajo	U.S. White	U.S. Black
0	0.1	0.7	0.1
1	0.6	0.6	1.3
2	0.7	0.6	1.1
3	0.9	0.8	1.3
4	1.1	1.2	1.7
5	1.8	2.0	2.5
6	3.0	3.8	4.0
7	9.7	10.6	8.7
8	48.8	38.7	34.9
9	31.5	39.9	41.7
10	0.7	1.6	1.5
% unknown	1.0	1.6	1.4

*Source: National Center for Health Statistics, 1985 Natality Statistics, p. 269.

No beneficial effect of early prenatal care or deleterious effect of late prenatal care could be observed among Navajo births (Table 17). Virtually the same proportions of infants were born with low and high 1-minute Apgar scores, regardless of when prenatal care was initiated.

TABLE 17

Apgar Scores by Trimester of First Prenatal Care
Navajo Births, 1983–1986

Apgar Score	Trimester Prenatal Care Began		
	First	Second	Third/None
<=4	3.1	3.3	3.8
5–6	4.9	4.4	5.0
7–8	58.3	60.5	59.2
9–10	33.6	31.8	32.0

There were slight differences in Apgar scores by age of mother: 4.2% fewer Navajo mothers aged 40 and over deliver babies with 1-minute Apgar scores of 9 or 10, compared to mothers under age 20 (Table 18). Conversely, 2.1% more older mothers delivered babies with Apgar scores of 4 or less, compared to the youngest age group.

TABLE 18

One Minute Apgar Scores by Age of Mother
Navajo Births, 1983–1986

Apgar Score	Age Group of Mother			
	<20	20–29	30–39	40+
	Percent Distribution			
<=4	3.0	3.3	4.0	5.1
5–6	4.3	4.8	5.4	6.6
7–8	59.7	59.0	58.7	59.4
9–10	33.0	32.9	31.9	28.8

Birth weight has a large effect on Apgar scores (Table 19). Ninety-three percent of normal weight infants had Apgar scores above 7, compared to 73% of low birth weight infants.

TABLE 19

One and Five Minute Apgar Scores for Low
and Normal Birth Weight Infants
Navajo Births, 1983-1986

Apgar Score	Low Birth Weight Percent		Normal Birth Weight Percent	
	1-min.	5-min.	1-min.	5-min.
<=4	15.7	5.3	2.7	0.4
5–6	11.0	5.1	4.6	0.5
7–8	52.6	25.7	59.4	9.7
9–10	20.6	63.9	33.3	89.4

Summary

In this chapter, three main points are highlighted. First, Navajo fertility is high, resulting in high rates of natural increase; earlier reductions in fertility seem to have halted. Second, nearly half the births are to single women, and teen pregnancies account for 17% of all births. Third, despite the less than optimal utilization of free prenatal care services and the relative economic and educational disadvantage of the population, birth outcomes are remarkably favorable in terms of the incidence of low birth weight infants and Apgar scores.

A number of plausible explanations exist for the third finding. Perhaps Navajo women engage in or refrain from certain behaviors, which results in the birth of healthy infants. Perhaps the Indian Health Service has performed a virtual miracle in delivering quality services to this population. It is also possible that previous harsh conditions within this population have selected only the fittest for survival, and that the survivors of past adversity now enjoy a genetic advantage over other childbearing populations.

The single childbearing pattern that we observed can be understood within the biosocial framework outlined by Lancaster (1989). This leaves us with the question of extant high fertility. This investigation provides little evidence of imminent or in progress fertility decline. However, the current rate of natural increase and the present inadequacy of the land, resource, and economic bases will be pushing the traditional Navajo way of life up against Malthusian limits. It is inconceivable that radical change of some sort will not accompany a doubling of the population in little over a quarter of a century. The demographic options are three: fertility must decline, mortality must rise, or migration must occur. Some combination of the three is likely. I shall return to these options in the final chapter, and attempt to synthesize the results of this inquiry with the theoretical perspectives outlined in Chapter 2.

Chapter **5**

MORTALITY: AN OVERVIEW

There are striking differences in both the absolute levels of mortality and the patterns of death between males and females. The risk of death in males is nearly double that of females (risk ratio = 1.89). Sixty-four percent of all Navajo deaths during this time period occurred in males; 34% in females.

The crude death rates by sex for Navajos and other comparison groups are presented in Figure 34. This bar graph would seem to imply that Navajos have the lowest mortality of all the groups, but the largest disparity between men and women. However, the youthful age of the Navajo population, resulting from high fertility, makes this figure misleading. The disparity between males and females is real, but Figure 35 presents the mortality rates adjusted for age, and shows Navajo males to be at the highest risk of dying.

Figures 36 and 37 show the five leading causes of death for male and female Navajos and all Indians as a percentage of deaths. Tables 20 and 21 present the crude rates for the ten leading causes of death in males and females.

Accidents are the leading cause of death for both Navajo males and females. Accidents are the fourth leading cause of death for all Americans and comprise 4.5% of all deaths; accidents comprise 16 and 32% of deaths for Navajo females and males, respectively.

Accidents are followed by heart disease and cancer in both sexes, though their positions are reversed, and the fourth leading cause of death is the category "Symptoms, Signs, and

111

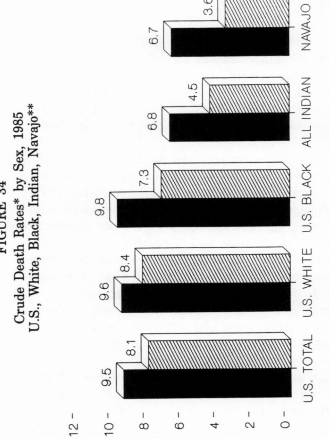

FIGURE 34
Crude Death Rates* by Sex, 1985
U.S., White, Black, Indian, Navajo**

*PER 1000 POPULATION
**ALL INDIAN 84-86 AVG, NAVAJO 83-86

■ MALE   ▨ FEMALE

	U.S. TOTAL	U.S. WHITE	U.S. BLACK	ALL INDIAN	NAVAJO
MALE	9.5	9.6	9.8	6.8	6.7
FEMALE	8.1	8.4	7.3	4.5	3.6

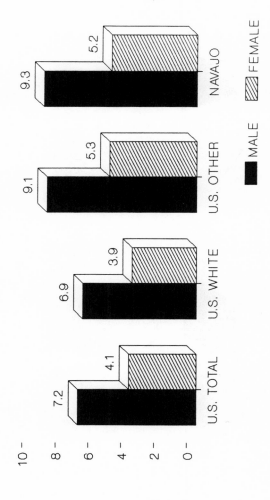

FIGURE 35

Age Adjusted Death Rates* by Sex, 1985
U.S., White, Other, Navajo**

*PER 1000 POPULATION, ADJUSTED
(DIRECT METHOD) TO 1940 U.S. POPULATION
**NAVAJO RATES 1983-86 AVERAGE

FIGURE 36
Five Leading Causes of Death
Indian Males

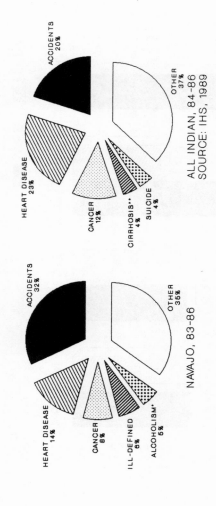

ACCIDENTS
20%

OTHER
37%

ALL INDIAN, 84-86
SOURCE: IHS, 1989

HEART DISEASE
23%

CANCER
12%

CIRRHOSIS**
4%

SUICIDE
4%

ACCIDENTS
32%

OTHER
36%

NAVAJO, 83-86

HEART DISEASE
14%

CANCER
8%

ILL-DEFINED
6%

ALCOHOLISM*
5%

*ICD9 291,303,571.0-571.3;**ICD9 571

FIGURE 37

Five Leading Causes of Death
Indian Females

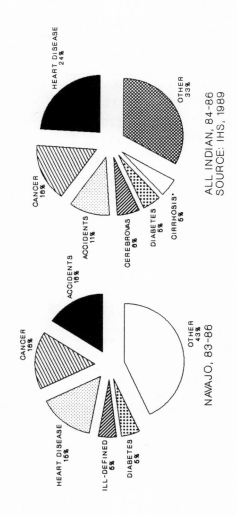

HEART DISEASE
24%

OTHER
33%

CANCER
16%

ACCIDENTS
11%

CEREBROVAS
6%

DIABETES
5%

CIRRHOSIS*
5%

ALL INDIAN, 84-86
SOURCE: IHS, 1989

CANCER
16%

ACCIDENTS
16%

HEART DISEASE
15%

ILL-DEFINED
6%

DIABETES
6%

OTHER
43%

NAVAJO, 83-86

*ICD9 571

TABLE 20

Ten Leading Causes of Death
Navajo Males Compared to All Indians

Cause of Death	Navajo 1983–1986		All Indians 1984–1986	
	Rank	CDR*	Rank	CDR*
All Causes	—	688.6	—	567.4
Accidents	1	217.0	2	112.8
(Motor Vehicle)		(135.3)		(61.1)
(Other)		(81.7)		(51.7)
Heart Disease	2	95.6	1	130.2
Cancer	3	53.0	3	69.1
Symptoms, Signs, Ill-Defined Conditions	4	39.7	Not Published	
Alcoholism**	5	33.3	4	24.0
Pneumonia/Influenza	6	28.4	8	19.2
Homicide	7	26.8	6	22.7
Suicide	8	26.5	5	23.0
Cerebrovascular Disease	9	17.1	7	20.8
Infectious/Parasitic Diseases	10	16.1	Not in Top Ten	

* Crude Death Rate per 100,000 population

** For Navajos: includes alcoholic psychosis, alcohol dependency syndrome, and alcoholic cirrhosis; for all Indians: includes chronic liver disease and cirrhosis (Source: IHS).

TABLE 21

Ten Leading Causes of Death
Navajo Females Compared to All Indians

Cause of Death	Navajo 1983–1986		All Indians 1984–1986	
	Rank	CDR*	Rank	CDR*
All causes	—	360.9	—	379.9
Accidents	1	58.4	3	41.6
(Motor Vehicle)		(40.7)		(24.5)
(Other)		(17.7)		(17.1)
Cancer	2	57.2	2	60.3
Heart Disease	3	54.8	1	90.4
Symptoms, Signs, Ill-Defined Conditions	4	19.5	Not Published	
Diabetes Mellitus	5	16.8	6	18.2
Pneumonia/Influenza	6	15.0	7	12.6
Alcoholism**	7	14.7	5	18.2
Cerebrovascular Disease	8	12.6	4	23.3
Infectious/Parasitic Diseases	9	11.7	Not In Top Ten	
Congenital Anomalies	10	9.6	10	6.8

*Crude Death Rate per 100,000 population
**For Navajos: includes alcoholic psychosis, alcohol dependency syndrome and alcoholic cirrhosis; for all Indians: includes chronic liver disease and cirrhosis (Source: IHS).

Ill-defined Conditions," death certificates that cannot be coded to a more specific cause from the information given. This catch-all code is commonly in the top ten causes of death in developing countries, and reflects the quality of health care available, the attention given to data collection, the prevalence of autopsy in the population, and other sociocultural factors. This cause of death is not ranked by the

National Center for Health Statistics, nor by the Indian Health Service because it does not reflect a real "cause" of death. It is ranked in this study because it is such a prominent category of death.

Completing the top ten causes of death for males are Alcoholism, Pneumonia and Influenza, Homicide, Suicide, Cerebrovascular Disease, and Infectious and Parasitic Diseases. The alcoholism category includes alcoholic psychosis, alcohol dependency syndrome, and alcoholic cirrhosis. This category of death is also not ranked by the NCHS. Only cirrhosis of the liver (alcoholic and non-alcoholic) is included in standard cause of death reports in the United States. It is reported and ranked in this study because of its contribution to total mortality. Other reports of mortality by cause often report only deaths coded to alcohol dependency syndrome under the alcoholism category, so comparisons may be misleading. The Indian Health Service publication (IHS, 1989) used for rate comparisons in Tables 20 and 21 includes chronic liver disease and cirrhosis.

The remaining top ten causes of death for females include Diabetes, Pneumonia and Influenza, Alcoholism, Cerebrovascular disease, Infectious and Parasitic Diseases, and Congenital Anomalies. Additional discussion of selected causes of death can be found in Chapter 7, "Cause Specific Mortality."

Figures 38–40 show the age specific mortality rates from all causes of death for Navajos, U.S. blacks, and U.S. total, presented on log scale. Of the three groups, Navajos show the greatest disparity between mortality in males and mortality in females, especially in the early and middle adult years.

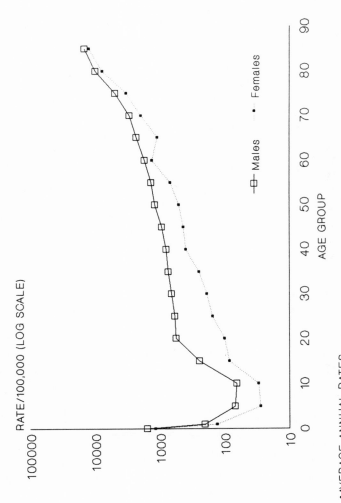

FIGURE 38

Age Specific Mortality Rates*
All Causes, by Sex, Navajos, 1983–1986

RATE/100,000 (LOG SCALE)

100000

10000

1000

100

10

0   10   20   30   40   50   60   70   80   90

AGE GROUP

🔲 Males   ••• Females

*AVERAGE ANNUAL RATES

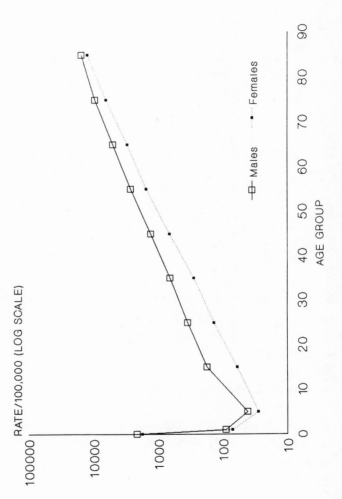

FIGURE 39
Age Specific Mortality Rates,
All Causes, by Sex, U.S. Blacks 1985

RATE/100,000 (LOG SCALE)

AGE GROUP

-□- Males   ····•···· Females

Source: NCHS

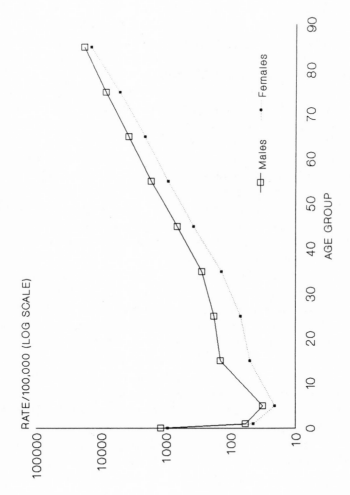

FIGURE 40

Age Specific Mortality Rates,
All Causes, by Sex, U.S. Total, 1985

RATE/100,000 (LOG SCALE)

100000

10000

1000

100

10

AGE GROUP

0   10   20   30   40   50   60   70   80   90

—□— Males   ····•···· Females

Source: NCHS

Life Expectancy

Life expectancy at birth for Navajo females is a respectable 77 years compared to 67 years for males (Table 22). Life expectancy for total U.S. females is 78, only one additional year; Navajo males lag three years behind life expectancy for U.S. males. Life expectancy for all Indians and Alaska Native females was 75.1 in the time period 1979–1981; for males it was 67.1 (IHS, 1984).

Table 22 also shows the changes in life expectancy since the early 1970s when Carr and Lee (1978) constructed life tables for Navajos. At each age, the average years of life remaining for males and females are shown, and the change between time periods. Life expectancies at birth for the years 1972–1974 were 59 years for males and 72 years for females. In slightly more than a decade, eight years have been added to the life expectancy of males and five to females. Males below the age of 50 have made larger gains in life expectancy than females from the earlier time period; over the age of 70 their losses have been greater.

In the earlier time period, the expectation of survival in the age group 1–4 years was greater than in the first year of life, reflecting higher infant mortality than in the later time period. However, life expectancy at older ages has declined for both sexes since 1972–1974. Males over the age of 70 and females over age 75 have fewer expected years of life remaining than a decade earlier. Perhaps small numbers in these age groups account for this unexpected finding, but it is consistent over the relevant age groups and for both males and females.

The earlier slight observed survival advantage of males over females in the oldest age group has also disappeared in the current series. This type of mortality crossover can be observed in some developing countries, and can be inferred to have been larger in Navajos in the past by comparing the sex ratios of males to females in the oldest age groups in earlier censuses. For example, in 1950, the ratio was 114 males 65 years or older to every 100 females, but in 1980 the ratio was 87:100 (Navajo Nation, 1988).

Tables 23 and 24 show, for males and females separately, how many years of life could be added at birth and at working ages if certain leading causes of death could be eliminated. The elimination of accidents would add almost six years of life to male Navajo life expectancy, while the elimination of cancer would add less than two. The differences between years of life added at birth and in working ages reflect the relative importance of a cause in childhood and in the retirement years compared to ages 15 to 65; they also reflect the economic impact of the various causes of death. For females, eliminating accidents as a cause of death would add only two years to life expectancy at birth, less than eliminating cancer or cardiovascular disease, but accidents remain the most important cause of death in working age men. Eliminating cardiovascular disease would add the most years, about four, to Navajo female life expectancy at birth.

Carr and Lee (1978) also calculated added years of life, eliminating leading causes of death, but the categories of death differ somewhat from those used in this study. They did find, however, that eliminating motor vehicle accidents would add the greatest number of years to male life expectancy at birth (5.17) and to the life expectancy of both males (3.11) and females (1.14) in the working ages.

TABLE 22

Life Expectancy by Age, Group, and Sex
Navajos, 1972–1974* and 1983–1986,
and Change Between Time Periods

| Age Group | Life Expectancy (Average Years Remaining) | | | | | |
| | Males | | | Females | | |
	72–74	83–86	Change	72–74	83–86	Change
0–1	58.84	66.83	7.99	71.83	77.12	5.29
1–4	59.63	66.88	7.25	72.39	77.03	4.64
5–9	56.11	63.41	7.30	68.98	73.42	4.44
10–14	51.27	58.62	7.35	64.14	68.52	4.38
15–19	46.53	53.80	7.27	59.24	63.62	4.38
20–24	42.70	49.43	6.73	54.67	58.88	4.21
25–29	39.48	45.78	6.30	50.44	54.16	3.72
30–34	36.97	42.06	5.09	46.13	49.56	3.43
35–39	33.73	38.38	4.65	41.83	45.00	3.17
40–44	30.80	34.73	3.93	37.81	40.53	2.72
45–49	27.61	31.04	3.43	33.98	36.29	2.31
50–54	27.89	27.39	−0.50	29.98	32.02	2.04
55–59	22.20	23.93	1.73	26.28	27.77	1.49
60–64	19.27	20.43	1.16	22.27	23.65	1.38
65–69	16.49	17.04	0.55	18.35	20.09	1.74
70–74	14.19	13.80	−0.39	14.74	16.08	1.34
75–79	12.30	10.59	−1.71	12.83	12.49	−0.34
80–84	10.23	7.86	−2.37	10.31	9.29	−1.02
> = 85	8.89	6.47	−2.42	8.64	7.60	−1.04

*Source: Carr and Lee, 1978

TABLE 23

Added Years of Life Eliminating Selected
Leading Causes of Death
Navajo Males, 1983–1986

Cause of Death	Added Years of Life	
	At Birth	Working Ages*
Accidents	5.95	3.65
(Motor Vehicle)	(3.67)	(2.49)
(Other)	(2.28)	(1.16)
Cardiovascular Disease	3.93	.80
Cancer	1.62	.46
Homicide and Suicide	1.40	.95
Alcoholism**	1.05	.70
Pneumonia and Influenza	.82	.12

*Ages 15–65
**Includes alcoholic cirrhosis, alcohol dependency syndrome and alcoholic
psychosis.

TABLE 24

Added Years of Life Eliminating Selected
Leading Causes of Death
Navajo Females, 1983–1986

Cause of Death	Added Years of Life	
	At Birth	Working Ages*
Accidents	2.10	.90
(Motor Vehicle)	(1.38)	(.70)
(Other)	(.72)	(.20)
Cancer	2.78	.72
Cardiovascular Disease	4.17	.46
Diabetes	.80	.17
Pneumonia and Influenza	.82	.05
Alcoholism**	.60	.35

*Ages 15–65
**Includes alcoholic cirrhosis, alcohol dependency syndrome and alcoholic
psychosis

Seasonality of Deaths

Table 25 shows observed and expected deaths by month, adjusted for the length of the month. A chi square goodness of fit test was performed to see if there were significant departures from expected, if there was no seasonality in mortality. The third column of Table 25 depicts that month's contribution to the chi square. A chi square of 23.37 (df=11) was obtained, statistically significant at the .05 level. This table suggests that, aside from December, April really is the cruelest month. Deaths in the early part of the year and during the summer months are approximately equal to the numbers expected. There are fewer than expected deaths in the fall months, but many more than would be expected in December, perhaps owing to the holiday season. There were no striking differences in the causes of death in April and December. As a proportion of deaths for each month, pneumonia and influenza deaths were more common in April, and suicide and homicide were more common in December. Accidents comprised 19.8% of April deaths and 22.0% of December deaths.

Place and Circumstances of Death

A majority of Navajo women die as inpatients in a hospital, nursing home, or other patient care facility (64.3%); for males only 44.3% die under these circumstances (Table 26). About 25% of males die in the emergency room, as an outpatient, or are dead on arrival at a patient care facility. More than one-fourth of men and 17% of women die in other places, such as the home.

TABLE 25

Seasonality of Deaths
Navajo Area, 1983–1986

Month of Death	Observed	Expected*	Contribution to Chi-Square
January	291	283.50	.20
February	263	256.06	.19
March	257	283.50	2.48
April	313	274.36	5.44
May	291	283.50	.20
June	278	274.36	.05
July	269	283.50	.74
August	288	283.50	.07
September	239	274.36	4.56
October	266	283.50	1.08
November	255	274.36	1.37
December	328	283.50	6.99
Total	3,338	3338.00	23.37

*Adjusted for length of month
Chi-Square Goodness of Fit (11df)=23.37, p<.05.

TABLE 26

Place and Circumstances of Death by Sex,
Navajo Area Deaths, 1983–1986

Place of Death	Male		Female	
	#	%	#	%
Hospital, Clinic, Medical Center	1,411	66.2	883	73.2
(In-Patient)	(852)	(40.0)	(681)	(56.5)
(Out-Patient/E.R.)	(209)	(9.8)	(88)	(7.3)
(Dead on Arrival)	(350)	(16.4)	(114)	(9.4)
Other Institution*	91	4.3	94	7.8
Other Places	615	28.8	210	17.4
Place/Status Unknown	15	0.7	19	1.6
Total	2,132	100.0	1,206	100.0

*Providing patient care, e.g., nursing home

Leading Causes of Death By Age Group

In this section, leading causes of death and mortality rates by cause and sex will be considered for age groups beyond infancy. Infant deaths are treated separately in Chapter 6. Tables 27–32 show the rates for the leading causes of death for Navajo males and females, and for all Indians and the U.S. total for both sexes combined. All the tables will be presented first, and a short discussion of major causes in each age group will follow. In these tables only the standard NCHS classifications are used to facilitate comparisons. Alcoholism and ill-defined deaths, considered separately in Chapter 7, are omitted.

Ages 1–14

For Navajos and all Indians, accidents comprise more than half the total mortality in this age group (Table 27). Accidents account for less than half the total U.S. mortality from ages one through fourteen. However, childhood injury death rates in the United States are considerably higher than in most other industrialized countries, including Sweden, The Netherlands, Japan, England and Wales, and Germany (NCHS, 1989). Canada and Australia had injury mortality rates similar to the U.S. in 1985. Navajo females are the only group for whom motor vehicle accidents are more significant than other accidents; their motor vehicle mortality rate is double that of other accidents. In the remaining groups, other accidents are of equal or greater importance.

Navajo children are 2.5 times more likely to die as children in the entire U.S. The U.S. total mortality rate for ages 1–14 is 33.8 per 100,000 compared to 83.0 in Navajos. Heart disease and congenital anomalies were the only "natural" leading causes of Navajo death in this age group, and combined they accounted for only 13% of deaths, or about 11 deaths per 100,000 children.

TABLE 27

Leading Causes of Death in Age Group 1–14 Years
Navajos by Sex, All Indians, and U.S. Total

Cause of Death	Navajos			All Indians	U.S. Total
	M	F	T		
Accidents	58.4	34.4	46.4	28.2	14.7
(MVA)	(26.6)	(22.9)	(24.7)	(14.0)	(6.9)
(Other)	(31.9)	(11.5)	(21.6)	(14.1)	(7.8)
Diseases of Heart	7.1	5.3	6.2	1.9	1.3
Congenital Anomalies	4.4	5.2	4.9	2.6	2.7
Homicide	5.3	0.9	3.1	2.1	1.6
Pneumonia & Influenza	2.7	1.8	2.2	1.0	0.7
Suicide	2.7	0.9	1.8	1.2	0.6
All Causes	107.1	59.1	83.0	48.2	33.8

TABLE 28

Leading Causes of Death in Age Group 15–24 Years
Navajos by Sex, All Indians, and U.S. Total

Cause of Death	Navajos			All Indians	U.S. Total
	M	F	T		
Accidents	239.4	50.2	141.5	91.6	48.4
(MVA)	(173.5)	(43.9)	(106.5)	(60.1)	(36.1)
(Other)	(65.9)	(6.3)	(35.1)	(31.5)	(12.3)
Homicide	45.7	6.3	25.3	20.3	12.1
Suicide	37.7	3.8	20.1	24.4	12.9
Cancer	9.4	8.8	9.1	3.2	5.4
All Causes	380.6	91.6	231.1	161.5	95.9

TABLE 29

Leading Causes of Death in Age Group 25–44 Years
Navajos by Sex, All Indians, and U.S. Total

Cause of Death	Navajos			All Indians	U.S. Total
	M	F	T		
Accidents	354.1	73.2	206.1	103.0	35.2
(MVA)	(253.7)	(59.7)	(151.5)	(61.8)	(20.4)
(Other)	(100.4)	(13.4)	(54.6)	(41.2)	(14.8)
Chronic Liver & Cirrhosis	42.1	25.6	33.4	31.9	5.9
Homicide	36.6	14.6	25.0	24.1	13.2
Cancer	12.2	36.6	25.0	18.2	27.1
Suicide	47.5	2.4	24.4	23.3	14.9
Diseases of Heart	31.2	18.3	24.4	22.7	21.1
All Causes	671.5	225.6	436.6	292.0	159.5

TABLE 30

Leading Causes of Death in Age Group 45–64 Years
Navajos by Sex, All Indians, and U.S. Total

Cause of Death	Navajos			All Indians	U.S. Total
	M	F	T		
Diseases of Heart	230.5	88.4	153.0	236.4	295.2
Cancer	165.1	182.0	174.3	179.3	309.0
Accidents	286.6	80.6	174.3	89.4	33.9
(MVA)	(140.2)	(6.8)	(89.3)	(44.6)	(15.3)
(Other)	(146.4)	(33.8)	(85.0)	(44.8)	(18.6)
Diabetes	53.0	62.4	58.1	47.4	17.4
Chronic Liver & Cirrhosis	65.4	39.0	51.0	73.6	28.8
All Causes	1236.6	657.7	921.0	886.5	897.3

TABLE 31

Leading Causes of Death in Age Group 65 and Over
Navajos by Sex, All Indians, and U.S. Total

Cause of Death	Navajos			All Indians	U.S. Total
	M	F	T		
Diseases of Heart	1301.8	773.4	1026.7	1359.1	2172.6
Cancer	643.9	534.9	587.1	664.2	1046.5
Pneumonia & Influenza	426.9	251.3	335.5	205.5	206.1
Accidents	461.0	135.3	291.9	129.0	87.5
(MVA)	(161.0)	(45.1)	(100.7)	(36.3)	(21.6)
(Other)	(300.9)	(90.2)	(191.2)	(92.7)	(65.9)
Cerebro-vascular	266.0	193.3	228.2	295.6	463.7
Diabetes	126.0	199.8	164.4	169.7	95.6
All Causes	4864.2	3396.5	4100.1	3812.6	5152.4

May (1987a) has suggested that parental vigilance, access to safe playing areas and home environment, and use of seat belts and child restraint devices would help decrease childhood mortality differentials in Indians.

Ages 15–24

The leading causes of death in this age group are all external causes of death, with the exception of cancer (Table 28). For Navajo males, accidents, homicide and suicide account for 85% of all deaths; for females, these causes account for 68.6% of deaths. Even in the US. as a whole, 78% of all deaths result from intentional or unintentional injury.

Death rates are approximately three times higher in this age group than in the age group 1–14, for all groups. They are three and a half times higher in Navajo males. In fact, young Navajo males in this age group are almost four times more likely to die than teens and young adults of both sexes in the total U.S.

Homicide and suicide rates are approximately double in the Navajo and all Indian group, compared to the U.S. total. Both affect males disproportionately. Homicide is seven times more likely and suicide is nine times more likely in Navajo males, compared to Navajo females. Homicide predominates over suicide in Navajos, whereas it is the reverse in the all Indian group. Rates for the total U.S. are about even.

Since almost all the deaths in this age group are potentially preventable, effective intervention programs could substantially lower mortality rates in this age group. It is likely that the same high risk behaviors observed across racial groups would not be responsive to a single intervention program. Instead, culturally relevant interventions will probably be necessary.

Ages 25–44

Navajos in this age group have even higher accident rates than the previous age group (Table 29). By this age, the accident rates have declined in the entire U.S., and are essentially unchanged in the all Indian group. Motor vehicle mortality among Navajo males is more than ten times greater than for the U.S.

Chronic liver disease and cirrhosis makes its first appearance in this age group as a leading cause of death in Navajos and in all Indians. The rate for the U.S. is insignificant, approximately six deaths per 100,000. The rate for Navajo males is 42.1, seven times greater than the U.S. total. There are likely to be differences in reporting deaths attributable to this cause by ethnic group, however. This topic is explored in greater detail in Chapter 7.

Chronic liver disease and cirrhosis is not an insignificant cause of death for Navajo females, though. The rate exceeds that of other accidents, homicide, suicide, and diseases of the heart. Chronic liver disease and cirrhosis accounts for 6% of male deaths and 11% of female deaths. However, the ratio of male to female deaths is 1.64. In this age group, suicide rates are higher than homicide rates in males; both are low in females. Mortality from heart disease is higher (1.7 times) in Navajo males, compared to females.

Ages 45–64

In middle age, the leading causes of death in the Navajo begin to resemble the leading causes in the general population (Table 30). Males continue to have higher rates of heart disease, while females seem relatively protected. For males, heart disease is the leading cause of death; for females it is the third leading cause of death, behind cancer and accidents. Cancer is less common in Navajos and all Indians, compared to the U.S. total rate. In fact, accidents are equivalent to cancer mortality in this age group for both sexes combined. Motor vehicle accidents predominate in Navajo females, while other types of accidents are slightly higher in males.

Diabetes mortality is greater in the Navajo and all Indian population than in the U.S. A Navajo woman in this age group is 3.6 times more likely to die of diabetes than someone in the general U.S. population. Chronic liver disease and cirrhosis are again high in both Indian populations, but higher in the all Indian than in the Navajo group. For all causes of death the Navajo male is at increased risk, and the Navajo female is at decreased risk, of dying compared to the general population.

Ages 65 and Older

Heart disease is now the leading cause of death in both male and female Navajos of this age group, as in the general population (Table 31). The rate in Navajos is, however, half the rate for the total U.S. Cancer is the second leading cause of death in Navajos of both sexes, followed by pneumonia and influenza and accidents. Cerebrovascular disease is the fifth leading cause of death in this age group; in the U.S. total population, it is the third leading cause of death.

The age-specific death rate from all causes is lower than that for the U.S. in this age group. For all other age groups, it has been higher. Rates in Navajos exceed U.S. rates for pneumonia and influenza, accidents, and diabetes.

Summary

We have seen that males are at a survival disadvantage in every age group. This disadvantage is lowest in infancy and old age, and greatest in teens and young adults. Table 32 shows the ratio of male to female mortality rates by age group. For all ages combined, males have almost twice the risk of dying, but the ratio is 4.2 in the age group 15–24 and 3.0 in the age group 25–44.

TABLE 32

Male to Female Mortality Rate Ratios
All Causes by Age, Navajos 1983–1986

Age Group	Rate Ratio
< 1	1.3
1–14	1.8
15–24	4.2
25–44	3.0
45–64	1.9
65+	1.4
All Ages	1.9

Almost all the excess can be attributed to external causes of death: accidents, suicide, and homicide, and to a lesser extent, the direct effects of alcohol abuse. The same can be said for the excess of male deaths in those age groups within the larger U.S. society. However, U.S. white males do not have the same magnitude of survival disadvantage as Indians or blacks; they enjoy some measure of protection against early violent death.

In the entire U.S. in 1985, only 10% of all deaths occurred to persons under the age of 45; for American Indians and Alaska Natives, 33% of deaths were to persons under age 45 (IHS, 1989). For Navajos of both sexes, 44% of deaths were below this age, and for males 49%, nearly half, of all deaths occurred to persons younger than 45.

Chapter 6

INFANT MORTALITY

Navajo infant mortality differs little from that of the U.S., approximately eleven deaths in the first year of life per 1000 live births (Figure 41). In 1990, New Mexico Navajo infant mortality actually fell below that of the 1989 U.S. total, 9.3 vs. 9.8 deaths per thousand live births (New Mexico Department of Health, 1992). The gap between U.S. and Indian infant mortality was enormous in 1955 when the rates were 62.7 for all Indians, 87.8 for Navajos, and 26.4 for the entire United States (Figure 42). There is some evidence that the gap between Navajo and U.S. infant mortality was even larger before 1950.

Morgan (1973) studied one group of Navajo at Ramah, and reported infant mortality rates of 141/1000 live births for the period 1925–1939 and 133 for the period 1940–1949. These rates are large increases over rates in previous time periods: 60/1000 live births in 1890–1909 and 89 in 1910–1924 (Morgan, 1973). Kunitz (1983) suggests that the stock reduction program, the declining productivity of the land, and the Depression caused a general worsening of the Navajo economy and the nutritional status of the people. Despite these early high rates, the gap has progressively narrowed until there are virtually no differences in overall infant mortality.

Low infant mortality among the Navajo does not appear to result from higher rates of fetal mortality. Since 1908, New Mexico has had a statute requiring reports of all fetal deaths weighing more than 500 grams, regardless of gestational age.

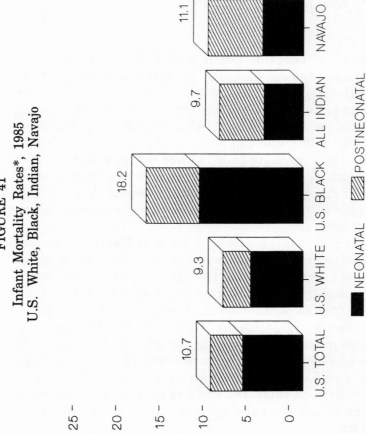

FIGURE 41
Infant Mortality Rates*, 1985
U.S. White, Black, Indian, Navajo

*Per 1000 Live Births

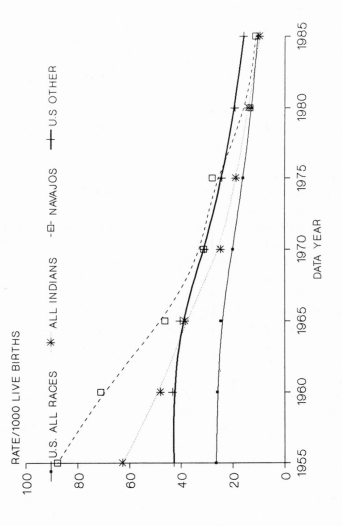

FIGURE 42
Infant Mortality Rates Since 1955
U.S. Total, Other, Indian, Navajo

Source Non-Indian Data: NCHS

Prior to that, reporting was required for deaths of 20 or more weeks gestation (New Mexico Health and Environment Department, 1990). For McKinley and San Juan counties (those encompassing the New Mexico portion of the Navajo reservation), the fetal death ratio per thousand live births was 4.7 and 6.3, respectively. The state total was 5.7 fetal deaths per thousand live births, compared to 8.0 in the entire U.S. in 1986 (New Mexico Health and Environment Department, 1990).

It may not be possible to untangle the role played by the IHS in reducing infant mortality from the role played by the general improvement in conditions on the reservation in the latter part of the 1950s. This is because reliable data are not available for the entire tribe in earlier time periods. However, Morgan's research (1973) suggests that infant mortality rates were sensitive to fluctuating conditions prior to the availability of IHS care. The role of IHS is an important question, even today, because the availability of free prenatal care may be one reason why Indian infant mortality is lower than black infant mortality. As we saw in Chapter 4, Navajo utilization of prenatal care is low, but has risen since the inception of IHS (Slocumb & Kunitz, 1977).

Differences between Indian and white infant mortality do emerge, however, in comparing neonatal to postneonatal infant mortality. Neonatal mortality refers to deaths occurring in the first 28 days, and postneonatal refers to the remainder of the first year of life. Navajo neonatal death rates were lower than U.S. neonatal rates. Postneonatal mortality was higher (6.3/1000) than neonatal mortality (4.8/1000), as has been reported in other studies (Broudy & May, 1983; Kunitz, 1989). Higher postneonatal mortality is thought to be related to the poor environmental conditions the infant is subjected to during the first year of life, while higher neonatal mortality is related to unfavorable conditions during pregnancy and childbirth, such as nutrition, drug use, short gestation, and low birth weight.

All indications point to the Navajo being a robust childbearing population. The incidence of low birth weight infants is lower than for U.S. whites (see Chapter 4). This is the proximate variable that probably accounts for the favorable neonatal death rate. On the other hand, Navajos are still disadvantaged in the home environment when it comes to the modern amenities, almost taken for granted, that most Americans have. Over half the homes on the reservation lack plumbing and piped water; three-fourths have no central heating or telephone; nearly one half lack electric lighting and refrigerators (Navajo Nation, 1988). Bringing an infant home from a hospital to live successfully under these conditions must surely involve the utmost in care and devotion. It is a wonder the postneonatal rates are as low as they are.

Table 33 shows more detailed information about the timing of infant deaths in Navajo males and females, compared to all Indians and the U.S. total. Over one-third of infant deaths among Navajo males and more than a fourth among females occur beyond the third month of life, in contrast to 13.3% of males and 14% of females in the total U.S. Eighteen percent of Navajo male infants who die do so after reaching six months of age.

The ratio of postneonatal to neonatal death is 1.3 for the time period 1983–1986, but it was much higher in earlier years, reflecting the even poorer environmental conditions existing at that time. For example, the ratio of postneonatal to neonatal death was 2.5 in 1955 and 2.3 in 1965 (Kunitz, 1989). Only since the 1970s have the neonatal and postneonatal rates achieved some parity, although both have declined dramatically since the 1950s.

As expected, male infant mortality was higher (12.5/1000) than female infant mortality (9.6/1000), reflecting the generally increased male susceptibility to death. Omran and Loughlin (1972) curiously report a higher female infant mortality rate for the Many Farms/Roughrock portion of the reservation in the late 1950s. The ratio of postneonatal to neonatal mortality was different for males and females. For females the ratio was 1.2, but for males it was 1.4. In fact, the postneonatal mortality rate for females was the same as the neonatal mortality rate for males (5.2/1000). This suggests that males are at an increased disadvantage, compared to females, in the home environment. In the next section, the specific causes that contribute to higher mortality among males will be explored.

TABLE 33

Percent Distribution of Infant Deaths
by Detailed Age at Death
Males and Females, U.S. Total*, All Indian**, Navajo

Age at Death	U.S. Total M	F	All Indian M	F	Navajo M	F
<1 Day	36.7	38.3	23.5	25.2	20.7	16.8
1–3 Days	13.7	13.0	8.6	9.9	7.1	14.8
4–6 Days	3.9	3.7	2.9	3.8	1.4	5.9
7–27 Days	10.7	10.8	10.2	11.1	12.1	7.9
1–3 Months	21.6	20.1	30.3	29.8	22.9	26.7
4–6 Months	8.1	7.8	13.3	11.9	17.9	14.9
>7 Months	5.2	6.2	11.1	8.4	17.9	12.9

*Adapted from NCHS
**Indian rates are averaged over the years 1983–1986.

Increasingly, the utility of using neonatal and postneonatal mortality rates as a proxy for endogenous (genetic and developmental) vs. exogenous (environmental) causes of infant death has been called into question (Poston & Rogers, 1985; Stockwell, Swanson & Wicks, 1987). Poston and Rogers found, in a New Mexico study, that endogenous and exogenous causes converged on the eighteenth rather than the twenty-eighth day. Stockwell, et al. found that endogenous causes predominated in both the neonatal (93% of deaths) and the postneonatal (73% of deaths) period, using data from Ohio. Moreover, as neonatal intensive care services become more and more elaborate, it is reasonable to assume that some deaths are being postponed to the postneonatal period or later, rather than being prevented. Whether the neonatal period should be shortened or extended, as suggested by the findings of these two studies, is unclear. It is becoming clear, however, that infant mortality patterns result from a complex interaction of biological, social, and environmental factors. Many of our previous assumptions about the determinants of infant mortality are being challenged by new data.

There was considerable variation in infant mortality rates by service unit (Figure 43). The Crownpoint and Fort Defiance areas had the highest rates (18.6 and 15.4, respectively). In Crownpoint, the largest part of the high rate was in postneonatal deaths; neonatal death rates were not elevated. In Fort Defiance, the situation was reversed: neonatal rates were elevated. These two areas are transition areas, characterized by rapid change, more wage work, and development. Kayenta, Chinle, and Shiprock, three traditional areas, had the lowest infant mortality rates.

Data from 1979 to 1981 (IHS, 1984) presented in Table 34 indicate that Chinle has experienced the most dramatic decline in infant mortality, from 22.1 to 7.0 in just a few years. During this time, a new hospital was built in Chinle, increasing accessibility to health care. Crownpoint and Fort Defiance have experienced the least decline. Rates for these areas were 22.3 and 16.5 in the 1979–1981 time period, and they declined to 18.6 and 15.3 in the 1983–1986 period.

Current infant mortality rates among Indians and rates over time contrast sharply with the observed pattern in blacks. African American infants have almost twice the risk of dying in the first year of life (Figure 41), and the neonatal rate is higher (12.1) than the total infant mortality rate for the U.S.! Again, it is primarily through the proximate determinant, low birth weight, that blacks are at increased risk of dying in the first four weeks of life.

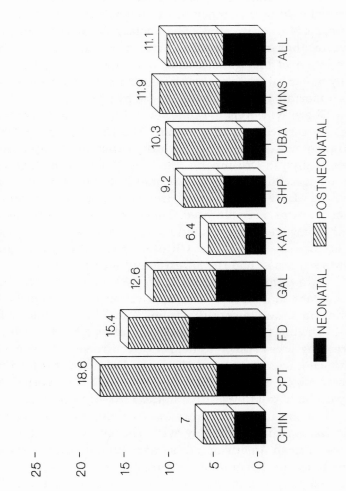

FIGURE 43

Infant Mortality Rates by Service Unit, Navajo 1983–1986

*PER 1000 LIVE BIRTHS

TABLE 34

Infant Mortality Rate* by Service Unit
Navajo Area, 1979–1981** and 1983–1986

	Year	
Service Unit	1979–81	1983–86
Chinle	22.1	7.0
Crownpoint	22.3	18.6
Ft. Defiance	16.5	15.3
Gallup	15.9	12.7
Kayenta	9.5	6.5
Shiprock	13.4	9.2
Tuba City	14.3	10.2
Winslow	17.1	12.0
Total	16.3	11.1

*Deaths per 1,000 live births
**Source: IHS Summary Tables: American Indian and Alaska Native Infant
Deaths by Cause and Age, IHS Service Area, by Area/Program Office and
Service Unit, 1979–1981, August 1984.

Another contrast important to consider is the much
lower rate of infant mortality in other ethnic groups in the
U.S. and in other developed nations. Asian groups in America
have total infant mortality rates that are half the U.S. rate. In
1985, U.S. Chinese had a rate of 5.3 and the Japanese 4.4.
These rates approximate those of Sweden and Japan
(Hartford, 1984). Regardless of the dramatic decline in infant
mortality, there is still much room for improvement.

Infant Mortality by Cause

Sudden infant death syndrome (SIDS) is the leading
cause of death in all Indians under one year of age,
comprising almost one-fourth of all infant deaths (Figure 44).
In Navajo infants, congenital anomalies are the leading cause
of death, followed by respiratory distress syndrome (RDS) and

other intrauterine or newborn respiratory conditions (IUNBR); SIDS is the third leading cause of death in Navajo infants, and it accounts for only 9.1% of deaths. Congenital anomalies and RDS/IUNBR are the second and third leading causes of death, respectively, in the all Indian group. Completing the five leading causes of infant death list for all Indians are labor and delivery complications, 8%, and respiratory diseases, 6%. For Navajos, the fourth and fifth leading causes of infant death are meningitis, 7%, and respiratory diseases, 6%. These five causes account for 69% of all Indian infant deaths, but only 57% of Navajo infant deaths.

The leading causes of death among Navajo infants in 1970 show a somewhat different pattern (Brenner, et al., 1974). In that year RDS led the list (17.6% of deaths), followed by gastroenteritis (15.7%), congenital malformations (14.8%), prematurity (12.0%), and infection (11.1%).

These causes of death were deduced, however, from hospital charts rather than from death certificates, and no ICD equivalents were offered in this article so that comparisons could be made. ICD coding has changed since 1970. Nevertheless, a few deductions are possible. First, meningitis is the only infectious cause of death that appears on the current list. In the 1983–1986 time period, meningitis accounts for 7% of infant deaths; in 1970, it caused 6.5% of infant deaths. The proportion of deaths from RDS was also virtually unchanged. It appears that infectious diseases as a cause of death in Navajo infants has diminished substantially since 1970. It also appears that congenital malformations account for a slightly greater proportion of deaths in the current time period, compared to 1970. This trend has also been reported by Berry, et al. (1987), comparing national data in 1980 to 1960.

FIGURE 44

Five Leading Causes of Indian Infant Mortality, 1983–1986

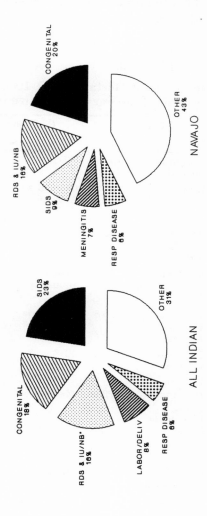

*Respiratory Distress Syndrome
& other Intrauterine/newborn
respiratory

Table 35 shows the top ten leading causes of infant death in the United States for 1985. The rates are also separated into neonatal and postneonatal categories. The following table, Table 36, compares male and female neonatal and postneonatal mortality rates among Navajos for 15 causes of death.

TABLE 35

Leading Causes of Infant Mortality, U.S. 1985
Neonatal and Postneonatal Rate Per 100,000 Live Births

Total		Neonatal		Postneonatal	
Cause	Rate	Cause	Rate	Cause	Rate
Congenital Anomalies	227.7	Congenital Anomalies	169.4	SIDS	131.2
SIDS*	141.3	RDS	90.9	Congenital Anomalies	58.3
RDS**	98.2	Short Gest./Low Birth Weight	85.8	Accidents	21.4
Short Gest./Low Birth Weight	86.6	Maternal Complications	35.0	Pneumonia/ Influenza	14.7
Maternal Complications	35.5	Intrauterine Hypoxia, Asphyxia	28.8	Septicemia	8.1
Intrauterine Hypoxia, Asphyxia	30.8	Perinatal Infection	24.3	RDS	7.2
Perinatal Infection	25.4	Placenta, Cord, Membrane	23.6	Meningitis	5.5
Placenta, Cord, Membrane	23.7	SIDS	10.2	Homicide	4.2
Accidents	23.7	Neonatal Hemorrhage	9.8	Bronchitis Bronchiolitis	2.7
Pneumonia/ Influenza	18.7	Birth Trauma	8.6	Neoplasms	2.3

* SIDS: Sudden Infant Death Syndrome
** RDS: Respiratory Distress Syndrome

TABLE 36

Neonatal and Postneonatal Infant Mortality Rates*
by Sex and Cause of Death
Navajo Area 1983–1986

	Males		Females	
Cause of Death	Neo	Post	Neo	Post
Infectious & Parasitic	—	71.46	—	38.10
Meningitis	—	62.53	—	85.71
Neoplasms	—	17.87	9.52	9.52
Respiratory Disease	17.87	53.59	—	38.10
Digestive System	—	71.46	9.52	47.62
Congenital Anomalies	160.79	62.53	142.86	76.19
Maternal Conditions	8.93	8.93	9.52	9.52
Labor, Delivery & Birth	62.53	—	38.10	—
RDS & Other Newborn Respiratory	169.72	26.80	133.33	19.05
Perinatal Infection	8.93	8.93	28.57	—
Other Perinatal	62.53	—	38.10	19.05
SIDS	17.87	125.06	—	57.14
Ill-Defined	—	35.73	9.52	19.05
Accidents	—	71.46	—	38.10
Homicide	8.93	17.87	—	—
All Others	—	98.26	19.05	66.67
Total	518.09	732.47	438.10	523.81

*Per 100,000 live births

For the major causes of death, perhaps it is easier to understand the relative importance of each cause among the comparison groups by examining Figures 45–54. This series of charts shows the rate/100,000 live births for the U.S. as a whole, whites, blacks, all Indians, and Navajos. A summary and discussion of the most important differences follows.

Congenital Anomalies

Deaths from congenital anomalies are similar for all groups, except in the all Indian group they are less common. The Navajo rate is 221.2 compared to the U.S. total rate of 227.7. This is in strong contrast to data presented in Chapter 4 showing that Navajo infants were almost three times more likely to have a congenital anomaly recorded on the birth certificate than the U.S. population. Table 37 shows the types of congenital anomalies fatal to infants in the first year, comparing Navajos and all Indians with the U.S. total. Navajos have lower proportions of respiratory, other CNS, and musculoskeletal anomalies, and higher proportions of hydrocephalus, genitourinary, other chromosomal and unspecified anomalies. Heart anomalies comprise one third of the congenital deaths in both the all Indian and Navajo groups. For Navajos, the "other chromosomal" category is the second most common fatal anomaly, while for all Indians, respiratory anomalies are.

Niswander, et al. (1975) studied major malformations among American Indians and found that, compared to Caucasians, Indians have a higher incidence of cleft lip and polydactyly, perhaps related to inbreeding, and a lower incidence of clubfoot and CNS abnormalities. Except for CNS abnormalities, the other malformations are not likely to cause death.

TABLE 37

Types of Congenital Anomalies Fatal in the First Year of Life
U.S. Total 1985, All Indians, Navajos 1983–1986

Type of Anomaly	U.S. Total #	U.S. Total %	All Indians #	All Indians %	Navajos #	Navajos %
Anencephalus	691	8.1	23	7.9	4	8.3
Spina Bifida	95	1.1	3	1.0	0	—
Hydrocephalus	203	2.4	5	1.7	2	4.2
Other CNS, Eye	274	3.2	11	3.8	0	—
Heart	2,585	30.2	100	34.1	16	33.3
Other Circulatory	689	8.0	28	9.6	4	8.3
Respiratory	1,094	12.8	31	10.6	1	2.1
Digestive	150	1.7	6	2.0	1	2.1
Genitourinary	509	5.9	15	5.1	4	8.3
Musculoskeletal	644	7.5	25	8.5	2	4.2
Down's Syndrome	74	0.9	6	2.0	1	2.1
Other Chromosomal	792	9.3	17	5.8	7	14.6
Other/Unspecified	761	8.9	23	7.9	6	12.5
Total	8,561	100.0	293	100.0	48	100.0

Respiratory Distress Syndrome

Respiratory Distress Syndrome (RDS) is less common in Indians compared to the U.S., and the rate is elevated in blacks (Figure 46). Maturational differences at birth (e.g., low birth weight) probably account for this pattern. As noted earlier, the proportion of RDS deaths among the Navajo has not changed since 1970 (Brenner, et al., 1974).

Sudden Infant Death Syndrome

Sudden Infant Death Syndrome (SIDS) is high in blacks and all Indians, suggesting a socioeconomic influence (Figure 47). However, Navajos appear to be somewhat protected. The rate in Navajo infants is less than for U.S. whites. Even if all

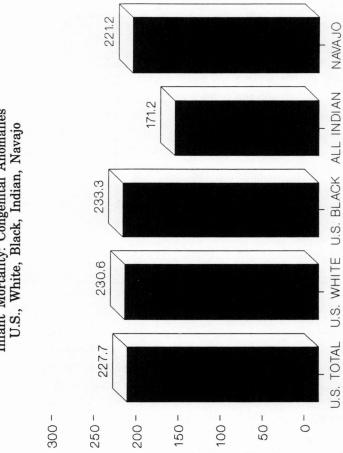

FIGURE 45

Infant Mortality: Congenital Anomalies
U.S., White, Black, Indian, Navajo

300 —

250 —

200 —

150 —

100 —

50 —

0 —

U.S. TOTAL   U.S. WHITE   U.S. BLACK   ALL INDIAN   NAVAJO

227.7   230.6   233.3   171.2   221.2

*PER 100,000 LIVE BIRTHS

Source Non-Indian Data: NCHS

FIGURE 46

Infant Mortality: Respiratory Distress Syndrome
U.S., White, Black, Indian, Navajo

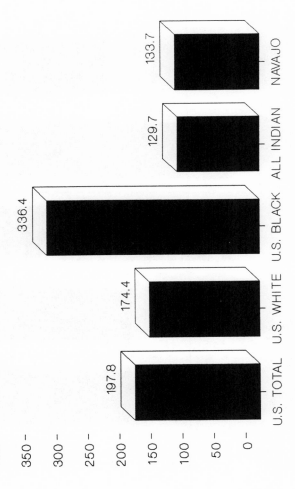

Source Non-Indian Data: NCHS

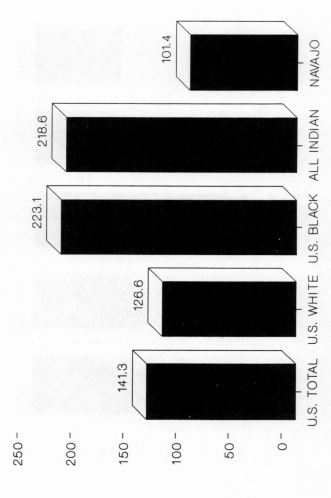

FIGURE 47
Infant Mortality: SIDS
U.S., White, Black, Indian, Navajo

141.3   126.6   223.1   218.6   101.4

U.S. TOTAL   U.S. WHITE   U.S. BLACK   ALL INDIAN   NAVAJO

*PER 100,000 LIVE BIRTHS

250 –
200 –
150 –
100 –
50 –
0 –

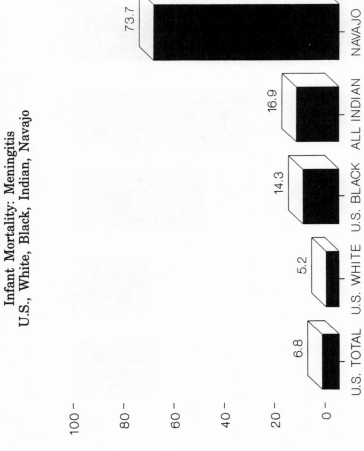

FIGURE 48

Infant Mortality: Meningitis
U.S., White, Black, Indian, Navajo

100 –

80 –

60 –

40 –

20 –

0 –

| 6.8 | 5.2 | 14.3 | 16.9 | 73.7 |

U.S. TOTAL   U.S. WHITE   U.S. BLACK   ALL INDIAN   NAVAJO

*PER 100,000 LIVE BIRTHS

Source Non-Indian Data: NCHS

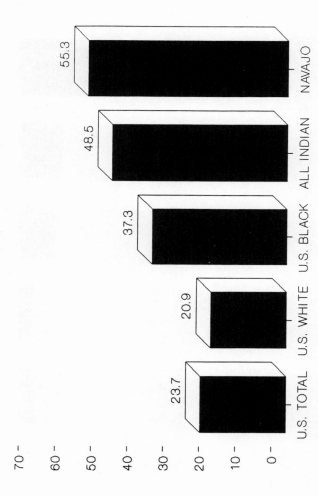

FIGURE 49
Infant Mortality: Accidents
U.S., White, Black, Indian, Navajo

*PER 100,000 LIVE BIRTHS

Source Non-Indian Data: NCHS

FIGURE 50

Infant Mortality: Infectious & Parasitic Diseases
U.S., White, Black, Indian, Navajo

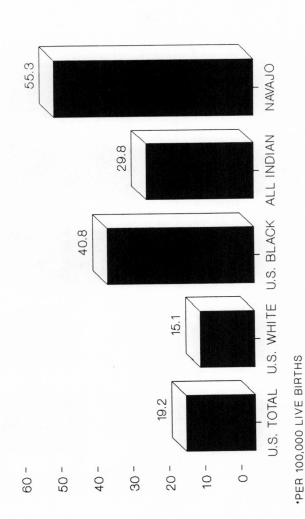

*PER 100,000 LIVE BIRTHS

Source Non-Indian Data: NCHS

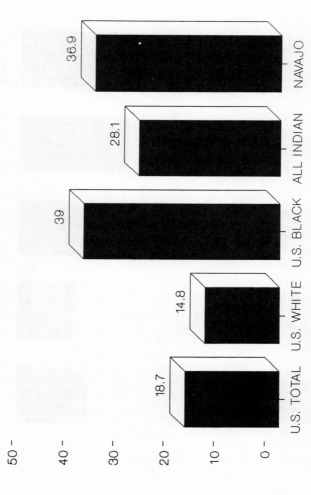

FIGURE 51

Infant Mortality: Pneumonia & Influenza
U.S., White, Black, Indian, Navajo

*PER 100,000 LIVE BIRTHS

Source Non-Indian Data: NCHS

FIGURE 52
Infant Mortality: Homicide
U.S., White, Black, Indian, Navajo

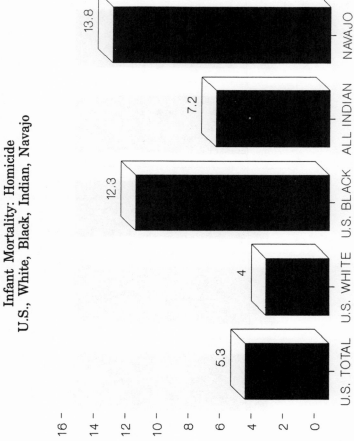

*PER 100,000 LIVE BIRTHS

Source Non-Indian Data: NCHS

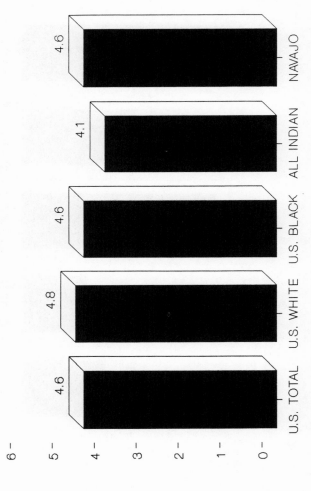

FIGURE 53
Infant Mortality: Neoplasms
U.S., White, Black, Indian, Navajo

*PER 100,000 LIVE BIRTHS

Source Non-Indian Data: NCHS

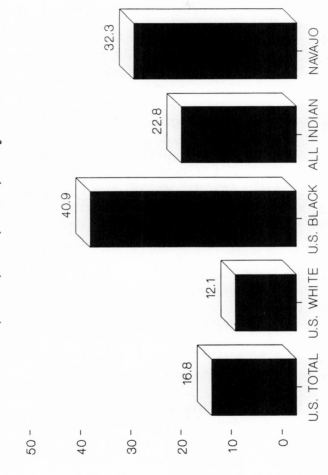

FIGURE 54

Infant Mortality: Ill-Defined Causes
U.S., White, Black, Indian, Navajo

*PER 100,000 LIVE BIRTHS; EXCLUDES SIDS

Source Non-Indian Data: NCHS

deaths from other ill-defined causes were added to the rate as a hedge against under-diagnosis of SIDS, the Navajo rate would still be lower than the U.S. total; black rates would be considerably elevated.

Investigators studying SIDS among Alaska Natives and Northwest Indians (Fleshman & Peterson, 1977; Bergman, et al., 1972; Kraus & Borhani, 1972) report even higher rates of SIDS among these populations: 454/100,000 in Alaska, 803 in Washington and 593/100,000 in California.

A subsequent study by Kaplan, et al. (1984) among Oklahoma Indians found lower rates of SIDS, 232/100,000 live births for the time period 1975–1981. This rate is comparable to the all Indian rate calculated from the 1983–1986 data of 219/100,000. The Alaska study (Fleshman & Peterson, 1977) also reported no excess of males, as most other studies have found. The male to female ratio reported by Kaplan, et al. (1984) was 1.75 among Oklahoma Indians; the rate in Navajo males was almost triple the rate for females (M/F ratio = 2.86).

Torrez (1990) found that Indian tribes in New Mexico with higher social disorganization had higher rates of SIDS than did tribes whose social organization was more intact. The relatively stable cultural practices of the Navajo may exert a protective effect on the risk of their offspring dying of SIDS.

Another study that examined ethnic- and cause-specific infant mortality in New Mexico also looked at birth weight as an independent variable, not just a control variable (Rogers, 1989). In general, low birth weight babies were at increased risk of dying from SIDS. However, even in the average birth weight categories, Anglos were twice as likely as Indians to die of SIDS, and were only at increased risk of SIDS (compared to Anglos and Hispanics) in the very low birth weight category (less than 1500 grams). As we observed in Chapter 4, the prevalence of low birth weight among Navajo women is relatively low. This factor alone may explain the favorable SIDS rate.

While the mysteries of SIDS will not be solved by this investigation, nor greatly illuminated, one point may bear further exploration. There seems to be tremendous variability in rates among groups with similar socioeconomic circumstances, and in some instances, genetic or cultural similarities. The fact that the excess in males ranges from nearly three times to almost nothing also seems important. Perhaps caretaking patterns in infancy, especially those which may affect males differentially, should be explored. Sleeping arrangements in the first six months of life might be one area that deserves additional investigation.

Meningitis

Meningitis does not appear to be a big problem for any group except the Navajo in the time period under investigation (Figure 48); it occurs exclusively in the post-neonatal period, presumably due to loss of the passive immunity acquired in utero through the mother (Coulehan, et al., 1984). Females have a higher rate than males (Table 36). A majority (60%) of the Navajo meningitis cases are caused by haemophilus B; another 20% by streptococcal pneumonia (May, 1987a; Coulehan, et al., 1984).

A larger proportion of haemophilus B meningitis cases occur in Navajo children under age 1 than in other populations (Coulehan, 1984). The recently introduced HIB vaccine should have already had an impact on Navajo childhood mortality from meningitis, and should be observable from more recent mortality statistics as they become available. Coulehan, et al. (1984) demonstrated that protective antibody titers could be obtained in Navajo infants 7–8 months of age by using PRP with the DPT vaccination schedule. However, this protection was obtained after the peak incidence of haemophilus influenza meningitis infection. Further studies may solve these problems and eliminate the last remaining infectious disease from the five leading causes of Navajo infant death.

Accidents

Accident rates are high among Indians in general, and highest among Navajos (Figure 49). Among the Navajo accidental deaths, one-fourth were caused by inhalation or ingestion of food or another object which caused respiratory obstruction or suffocation. Dissemination of information and demonstrations of the Heimlich maneuver might aid parents in coping with a common occurrence in infants beginning to eat solid foods. Timing of the introduction of solid foods into the infant diet is another area for potential exploration. The low telephone availability and long distances to medical services noted in Chapter 1 make this problem one that parents need to be knowledgeable in handling.

One-third of the accidental deaths were due to fires. Since the vast majority of homes lack central heating, it can be expected that wood burning and other flammable materials such as kerosene and propane would be more common in the household. The presence of these substances increases the probability of fire hazard. Omran and Loughlin (1972) found burns to be the leading cause of non-fatal injury in Navajo infants over the time period 1956 through 1962. Thus, this type of injury has posed a longstanding risk to Navajo infants.

The tribe could start a campaign to reduce fire deaths by purchasing many household type fire extinguishers and smoke alarms and making them available to families at a reduced cost, along with a well-publicized health education module.

Mortality from motor vehicle accidents is high in all Indians, Navajos in particular. Of the Navajo infant accidental deaths, 42% resulted from motor vehicle accidents. A large part of the rate is related to rural residence. Rural residence involves greater distance to desired destinations (work, shopping, leisure, and the emergency room) and the poorer condition of roads and communications. Infants riding with parents probably have longer exposure to the hazards of the road. In the case of the Navajo, there may be less use of infant car seats, and more children traveling with their parents in one vehicle. Family size is larger, and extended family groups may "carpool" into town for shopping or other activities, resulting in more persons per vehicle.

The pickup truck is ubiquitous on the Navajo reservation, practically a necessity considering the roads and weather conditions. Making room in the cab of a truck for an infant restraining device may seem unnecessary to many Navajo families, when doing so would mean another family member might have to stay home or ride in the truck bed. May (1987a) has suggested that tribal programs emphasizing seat belt use and restraining devices for children would reduce accident mortality in Indian youths.

Other Causes of Death

Infectious and parasitic diseases are higher in blacks and Navajos (Figure 50). Crowded dwellings and poor sanitary conditions are implicated. The rate for Navajos exceeds that of blacks.

Pneumonia and influenza rates follow the same pattern as infectious and parasitic diseases (Figure 51). However, in this instance, the rate is highest for blacks. This may reflect greater susceptibility in blacks following a higher prevalence of low birth weight accompanied by immaturity of the respiratory system, or the added assault of maternal smoking or urban air pollution in areas where the majority of blacks live.

Homicide in infancy is either a case of being an unwanted child, or being in the wrong place at the wrong time (Figure 52). Infants may be the real target of violence from a parent, step parent, or acquaintance, or they may die amidst violence surrounding them. Navajo and African American infants are at more than three times the risk of dying of homicide than U.S. white infants.

Alcohol abuse has been linked to the incidence of child abuse in several studies. White (1977) found that alcohol was related to 50% of abuse and 80% of neglect incident cases in his study of Navajos. Lujan, et al. (1989) found even more alcohol involvement in a southwestern Pueblo incidence study. They also found that the biological mother was most often the perpetrator of the abuse or neglect (40.2% of cases), or the mother and father together (32.4%).

These observations merit further investigation, with a final note of caution concerning the rates for Navajos. The rate is based on three cases over a period of four years, two of child battering and one other homicide. Additional years of data would be necessary to conclude that homicide rates are indeed elevated in Navajo infants.

Neoplasm rates show so little variation among the groups that it is difficult to postulate a differential genetic, environmental, or socioeconomic influence (Figure 53). The cancers found in adulthood will not follow this pattern.

Lastly, Figure 54 shows the rates of ill-defined causes of death for all the comparison groups. U.S. blacks have over three times the rate of U.S. whites. The Navajo rate is almost as high as the black rate.

Concluding Remarks

The infant mortality rate has been widely used as a sensitive indicator of the general well-being of a society. We see in the Navajo a curious mixed pattern, and the utility of infant mortality as a gauge of societal health must be called into question.

On the one hand, infant mortality rates have dropped precipitously in the last forty years and are now as low as the U.S. rate. Moreover, the Navajo appear to be a robust childbearing population, with few of the demographic indicators of socioeconomic disadvantage. Perhaps high mortality rates in the past have selected only the most robust for survival. On the other hand, patterns of death in infants do reflect the relatively harsh conditions of their environment, and many infant deaths are clearly preventable. It would be a mistake to view low rates of infant mortality as an indication that socioeconomic conditions are adequate, just as it is a mistake to hold poverty solely responsible for high rates of infant mortality, though many investigators have made this error in regard to black infant mortality rates.

Johnson (1987) marshals evidence from a number of studies of infant mortality "suggesting that cultural, social and biological factors may interact to create unique mortality patterns among racial and ethnic sub-groups" (p. 227). Untangling this web of interaction seems to be a worthy task that can lead to better intervention programs, and an eventual decline in infant mortality for all groups. This task must take into consideration both the neonatal/postneonatal differences and differences by birthweight and cause of death, as well as the standard control variables, such as the mother's age, education, marital status, and interbirth interval.

With respect to the Navajo, neonatal rates are low, but they could potentially be lower. Utilization of prenatal care services is also low. As has been reported for the Hispanic population, infant mortality remains low regardless of when, or if, prenatal care is begun (Johnson, 1987). The deleterious effects of single childbearing on infant mortality appear to be modified by ethnicity and age as well (Johnson, 1987). Babies born to single, black and teen mothers are not at increased risk of dying in the first year of life, compared to either older single mothers or married teen mothers. These findings cannot formally be tested on the Navajo from the current data because the birth and death certificates are not linked. However, such a study should be undertaken in the future. Since half the Navajo births are to single mothers, and since childbearing begins early while infant mortality remains low, it is likely that researchers will confirm for the Navajo the pattern found in blacks.

Eberstein, et al. (1990) recently published an article that examines interactions between an array of socioeconomic and demographic variables and cause of death in infant mortality cases in Florida. Their findings emphasize the importance of both biological and socioeconomic factors. Just as there are interactions among the socioeconomic variables themselves, as reported above, these interactions produce different patterns as well as levels of mortality. For example, Eberstein, et al. (1990) found that later prenatal care was associated with higher rates of SIDS, and that low levels of education were important only in infectious and perinatal causes of death.

A fascinating prospective study by Boyce, et al. (1986) deals with pregnancy complications among Navajo women. These researchers found that the most traditional women had twice the rate of pregnancy complications as the least traditional women, controlling for conventional obstetric risk factors and independent of the timing of prenatal care. This finding is somewhat contradictory to what I would have expected, given that traditional areas had the lowest rates of infant mortality. The authors suggest that traditional Navajo women may be increasingly isolated from social support systems which, in turn, adversely affects the course of pregnancy. But it is these traditional women whom we would predict would be most closely linked to family and female kin. Even though Boyce, et al. did not study infant mortality per se, the link between pregnancy complications and infant mortality is direct and obvious.

In summary, the most recent studies of infant mortality point to extremely complicated interactions among social, cultural, medical, economic, and biologic variables. Explaining higher rates of infant mortality by way of economic disadvantage is no longer useful because of the wide variation in rates among similarly disadvantaged groups. In earlier time periods, infant mortality rates were much higher, and environmental conditions were the overwhelming cause of infant death. Now, rates are at much lower levels, and the cultural and perhaps biologic interactions are just becoming visible.

Before leaving the topic of infant mortality, the question of whether lowering infant mortality has a direct effect on fertility must be raised. The assumption that it reduces the demand for "insurance babies" has been an integral aspect of many population programs in Third World countries. In the Navajo, we see a pattern of unusually low, by Third World standards, infant mortality rate coupled with fertility equivalent to that of India. Childhood and early adult mortality in males remain high by Western standards, so it is possible that expectation of the deaths of some offspring could contribute to increased demand for children. However, if such a link is hypothesized, it needs to be tested directly. Other factors appear to have more explanatory potential, and these will be discussed in the concluding chapter.

Chapter **7**

CAUSE SPECIFIC MORTALITY

In this chapter, several leading causes of death among the Navajo will be considered individually. Tables 38 and 39 show the crude and age-adjusted rates for each of these causes of death for Navajo males and females. Additional information about each cause will be presented as it is discussed.

Perhaps a better understanding of these causes of death can lead to more informed policies and preventive measures. Many of the leading causes of death are not easily "cured" by modern medical techniques, nor is it likely that medicine, as we know it, will be very successful at "treating," or in some cases "naming" some of these problems. The solutions will have to come further "upstream" (McKinlay, 1974). As we review these mortality statistics and patterns, I encourage the reader to ponder with me what "upstream" measures might be appropriate.

Accidents

Accidents are clearly the Navajo's number one health problem. They are the leading cause of death for all ages combined, and are present on the list of leading causes of death in every age group. Motor vehicle accidents predominate in all but the oldest age group. The accident mortality rate in Navajos is almost four times that of the nation for males and 2.4 times for women.

TABLE 38

Average Annual Crude and Age Adjusted* Mortality Rates for
Leading Causes of Death, Navajo Males 1983–1986

	Mortality Rate	
Cause of Death	Crude	Age Adjusted
All Causes	674.0	857.9
Motor Vehicle Accidents	132.5	151.7
Other Accidents	80.0	99.1
Cardiovascular Disease	111.9	157.4
Cancer	52.2	78.4
Alcoholism	32.6	50.0
Diabetes	13.0	22.0
Pneumonia & Influenza	27.8	34.0
Homicide	25.9	28.1
Suicide	25.9	31.0
Symptoms, Signs, Ill-Defined	38.9	48.9
Infectious and Parasitic	15.8	19.8

*Adjusted to the total U.S. population, 1940,

TABLE 39

Average Annual Crude and Age Adjusted* Mortality Rates for
Leading Causes of Death, Navajo Females 1983–1986

Cause of Death	Mortality Rate	
	Crude	Age Adjusted
All Causes	357.2	465.7
Motor Vehicle Accidents	40.3	43.4
Other Accidents	17.5	20.7
Cardiovascular Disease	69.0	95.5
Cancer	56.6	84.6
Alcoholism	14.5	20.8
Diabetes	16.6	26.4
Pneumonia & Influenza	14.8	18.9
Suicide	1.8	1.7
Symptoms, Signs, Ill-Defined	19.3	24.7
Infectious and Parasitic	11.6	15.4

*Adjusted to the total U.S. population, 1940

As we saw in Chapter 5, eliminating all accidents as a cause of death would add six years to the life expectancy at birth for males, and two years to female life expectancy.

Tables 40 and 41 detail the life expectancy effects at each age group of eliminating motor vehicle accidents as a cause of death in Navajo males and females in two time periods. Data from the earlier time period (1972–1974) are from life tables constructed by Carr and Lee (1978). Identical methods are used for the later (1983–1986) time period. Also included in these tables are columns showing the number of

TABLE 40

Life Expectancy and Potential Years Gained by Eliminating
Motor Vehicle Accidents as a Cause of Death,
Navajo Males 1972–1974* and 1983–1986

| Age Group | Life Expectancy | | | |
	1972–74	Potential Gain	1983–86	Potential Gain
0–1	64.01	5.2	70.50	3.7
1–4	64.93	5.3	70.58	3.7
5–9	61.31	5.2	66.99	3.6
10–14	56.43	5.2	62.16	3.5
15–19	51.62	5.1	57.32	3.5
20–24	47.32	4.6	52.69	3.3
25–29	43.20	3.7	48.45	2.7
30–34	39.87	2.9	44.16	2.1
35–39	36.22	2.5	40.03	1.7
40–44	32.90	2.1	35.93	1.2
45–49	29.50	1.9	31.92	0.9
50–54	26.65	−1.2	28.09	0.7
55–59	23.61	1.4	24.42	0.5
60–64	20.40	1.1	20.83	0.5
65–69	17.19	0.7	17.37	0.3
70–74	14.80	0.6	14.09	0.3
75–79	12.80	0.5	10.84	0.2
80–84	10.79	0.5	7.98	0.1
85+	9.22	0.3	6.50	0.0

*Source: Carr and Lee, 1978

TABLE 41

Life Expectancy and Potential Years Gained by Eliminating
Motor Vehicle Accidents as a Cause of Death,
Navajo Females 1972–1974* and 1983–1986

| Age Group | 1972–74 | Life Expectancy | | |
		Potential Gain	1983–86	Potential Gain
0–1	74.53	2.7	78.50	1.4
1–4	75.09	2.7	78.42	1.4
5–9	71.49	2.5	74.67	1.3
10–14	66.62	2.5	69.72	1.2
15–19	61.69	2.4	64.79	1.2
20–24	56.92	2.3	59.91	1.0
25–29	52.42	2.0	55.07	0.9
30–34	47.84	1.7	50.29	0.7
35–39	43.38	1.6	45.60	0.6
40–44	39.14	1.3	40.99	0.5
45–49	35.11	1.1	36.69	0.4
50–54	30.97	1.0	32.37	0.4
55–59	27.10	0.8	28.05	0.3
60–64	23.04	0.8	23.87	0.2
65–69	19.07	1.4	20.27	0.2
70–74	15.43	0.7	16.25	0.2
75–79	13.49	0.7	12.63	0.1
80–84	10.80	0.5	9.43	0.1
85+	8.96	0.3	7.60	0.0

*Source: Carr and Lee, 1978

years which could be added to the life expectancy if motor
vehicle accidents were eliminated. The potential gain was
larger in the earlier time period; it was larger for males than
females in both time periods. Eliminating motor vehicle
accidents as a cause of death would have added 5.2 years to
the life expectancy of males at birth in 1972–1974, but only
3.7 years in 1983–1986. For females, the gain in life
expectancy at birth was reduced from 2.7 years to 1.4 years.
Overall improvements in life expectancy in the later time
period exceed what would have been expected had motor
vehicle accidents been eliminated in the earlier time period.
For males aged 50–54 in the 1972–1974 time period, it
appears that eliminating motor vehicle accidents would
actually reduce life expectancy, but this may either be an
artifact of small numbers or an error in the published data.

    In Figures 55 and 56 we see the large gap in age
specific motor vehicle accident mortality rates between
Navajos and the other comparison groups, even on the log
scale. The all Indian comparison group follows the same
general age pattern as the Navajo, but at a lower rate for both
sexes. The MVA mortality rate is lowest among children aged
5–14 for all groups and both sexes.

    It is interesting to note that U.S. black male MVA
mortality generally exceeds that of U.S. whites. However,
both male and female white mortality is higher in the 15–24
group, undoubtedly reflecting greater access of white youths
to vehicles.

    Navajo males have over three times the number of
motor vehicle fatalities as females (Figure 57). For Navajo
females, one-car crashes are the largest category, and
comprise one-third of MVA deaths. Pedestrian vehicle
accidents account for one-fourth of all MVA deaths. In males,
the proportions are reversed. One-third of all MVA deaths in
males result from pedestrian incidents, while one-car crashes
comprise one-fourth of the deaths.

FIGURE 55
Male Motor Vehicle Mortality
Age Specific Rates

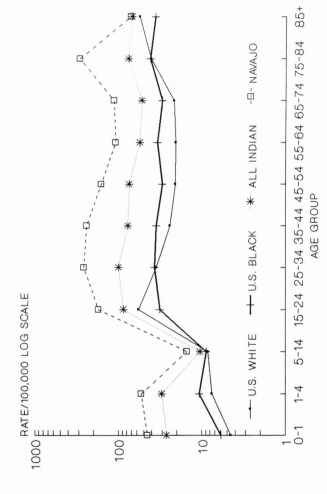

RATE/100,000 LOG SCALE

1000

100

10

1

0-1 1-4 5-14 15-24 25-34 35-44 45-54 55-64 65-74 75-84 85+

AGE GROUP

-•- U.S. WHITE   -+- U.S. BLACK   ...*... ALL INDIAN   -□- NAVAJO

U.S. DATA, 1985; SOURCE: NCHS
INDIAN DATA 1983-86 AVG.

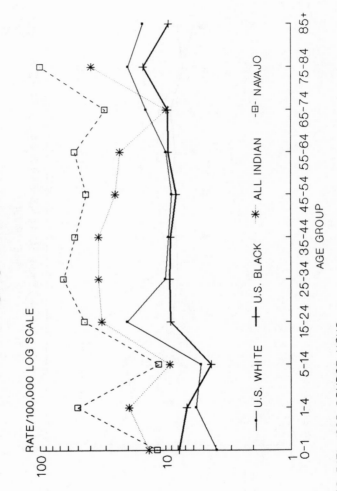

FIGURE 56
Female Motor Vehicle Mortality
Age Specific Rates

RATE/100,000 LOG SCALE

AGE GROUP

0-1 1-4 5-14 15-24 25-34 35-44 45-54 55-64 65-74 75-84 85+

— U.S. WHITE   —+— U.S. BLACK   ⋯*⋯ ALL INDIAN   -☐- NAVAJO

U.S. DATA, 1985; SOURCE: NCHS
INDIAN DATA 1983-86 AVG.

FIGURE 57

Motor Vehicle Accidents by Type
Navajo Males and Females

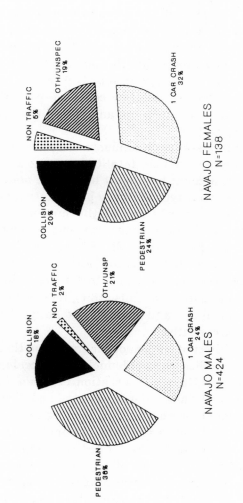

COLLISION
18%

NON TRAFFIC
2%

OTH/UNSP
21%

PEDESTRIAN
36%

1 CAR CRASH
24%

NAVAJO MALES
N=424

NON TRAFFIC
5%

OTH/UNSPEC
19%

COLLISION
20%

PEDESTRIAN
24%

1 CAR CRASH
32%

NAVAJO FEMALES
N=138

Age-specific mortality rates from other accidents do not follow exactly the same pattern as motor vehicle accidents (Figures 58 and 59). Navajo male rates are again higher than all other rates. The same dip in rates in the 5–14 age group also occurs, but beyond this age, mortality rates edge upward. Navajo female rates are not consistently higher than the all Indian and U.S. black groups, but they are consistently higher than U.S. whites at every age group. U.S. white rates are lower than all others, except they converge with the U.S. black rate in the 15–24 age group, and exceed the black rate in the oldest age group.

Other and late effects of accidents comprise the largest category of non-motor vehicle fatalities among the Navajo (Figure 60). These account for almost half of the male deaths, and it is unknown what type of injury precipitated the death. Again, male deaths greatly exceed the number of female deaths. Drowning is the next largest category of male deaths (20%), followed by fires and falls (8% each). Poisonings, railroad incidents, and choking or suffocation each accounted for 6% of other accidental deaths. In females, the second largest category of deaths was falls (18%), followed closely by fires (16%). Drownings and choking or suffocation each accounted for 11% of deaths.

Omran (architect of epidemiologic transition theory) and Loughlin (1972) studied the epidemiology of accidents on a small portion of the Navajo reservation between 1956 and 1962. Fatal and non-fatal accidents were studied. During this time period, accidents were the third leading cause of death overall, behind gastroenteritis and pneumonia. However, accidents were the leading cause of death in adults and the leading cause of death in males of any age. Alcohol use was associated with half the accidental deaths, and violence with nine percent of deaths. Omran also concludes that environmental hazards, poor condition of vehicles and driving skills contributed to accident fatalities. The authors suggest that the accident pattern among Navajos is more similar to

FIGURE 58

Male Other Accident Mortality
Age Specific Rates

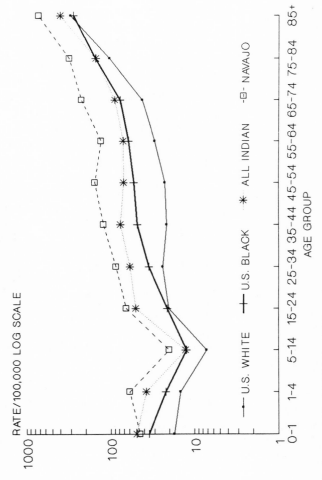

U.S. DATA, 1985; SOURCE: NCHS
INDIAN DATA, 1983-86 AVG.

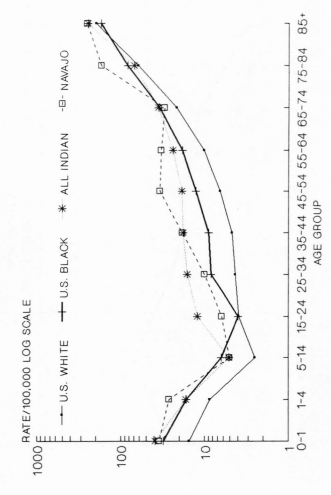

FIGURE 59
Female Other Accident Mortality
Age Specific Rates

RATE/100,000 LOG SCALE

— U.S. WHITE   —+— U.S. BLACK   —*— ALL INDIAN   —□— NAVAJO

AGE GROUP

U.S. DATA, 1985; SOURCE: NCHS
INDIAN DATA, 1983-86 AVG.

FIGURE 60

Other Accidents by Type
Navajo Male and Female

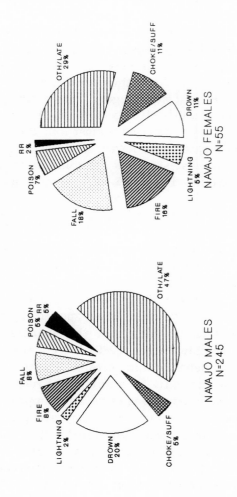

NAVAJO MALES
N=245

NAVAJO FEMALES
N=55

the pattern in Punjab, India, than to non-Indian communities surrounding the reservation.

Brown, et al. (1970) also studied the epidemiology of accidents on the Navajo reservation in 1966–1967. They found accident mortality double that of the nation, and a male to female ratio of approximately 3:1. For males, the lowest rate of accidents were in the 5–14 age group, just as in the current data. Motor vehicle accidents were the largest category of accident fatalities, and of these, the pedestrian motor vehicle accident was the largest subcategory. Interestingly, motor vehicle accidents comprised only 19% of the accidental injuries, whereas they comprised almost half the fatalities. Even though death rates were lowest in children aged 5–14, incidence rates were highest in this age group. In fact, school-aged children accounted for 46% of the total number of accidents.

Approximately one-third of the accidents occurred in or around the home. Thus, we see a rather stable portrait of accidents among the Navajo over time. If health education measures have been implemented, they do not seem to have altered the picture greatly.

At this point, I would like to raise some questions about the nomenclature we have been using, specifically the term "accident." This term implies that the event is beyond anyone's control (Christopherson, 1989), thereby removing the direct link between behavior and outcome. The term "injury" has been advocated recently by a number of researchers in this field. The word injury leaves us with the impression that these events are not random, that they are preceded by specific behaviors, and most importantly, that there is a potential for intervention (Christopherson, 1989).

Historically, it has been easier to focus the public attention on diseases than on injury although there are only three diseases that outnumber injury deaths, and these only beyond age 45 (Baker, O'Neill & Karpf, 1984). Despite this, injury control research has received little federal funding, only a fraction of what is spent on cancer and heart disease research (Christopherson, 1989). When we use the word injury rather than accident, it becomes clear that homicide and suicide are also injury deaths. What separates them from some, but not all, "accidents" is the intentional nature of the injury. Injury mortality, viewed in this more encompassing definition, clearly becomes the single most important health problem of the Navajo. Table 42 shows the number of cases of each type of injury mortality for males and females for 1983–1986.

There are three types of approaches to injury control. First, laws and regulations can be passed making certain high-risk behaviors illegal. An example of this would be seat belt legislation, which has certainly impacted motor vehicle fatalities. Second, people can be protected passively. Examples of this type of approach include road and vehicle designs, lighting, and other external or environmental manipulations. These do not require people's behavior to change, but lessen the consequences of behaviors. Third, people can be persuaded to change their behaviors, under some circumstances. For example, Christopherson (1989) discusses how expectant parents are more receptive to health education messages aimed at protecting infants and children than parents who already have young children. These parents may have developed a false sense of security by not having experienced any adverse effects. In considering how best to reduce injury mortality, all three approaches should be evaluated with regard to specific risk taking behaviors and within the age, sex, and culture of the groups to be targeted.

Suicide

Available historic information suggests that suicide rates among the Navajo were quite low in the distant past, moderately low in the recent past, and began a precipitous rise in the 1970s (Wyman & Thorne, 1945; Levy, 1965; Levy &

TABLE 42

Injury Deaths by Sex and Type of Injury
Navajo Area Deaths, 1983–1986

Type of Injury	Male		Female	
	#	%	#	%
UNINTENTIONAL INJURIES	672	78.1	194	84.7
Railway	12	1.4	1	0.4
Motor Vehicle (Total)	424	49.3	138	60.3
Collision	75	8.7	28	12.2
Pedestrian	152	17.7	33	14.4
Single Vehicle Crash	101	11.7	44	19.2
Other/Unspecified	88	10.2	26	11.4
Non-Traffic	8	0.9	7	3.1
Poisoning	12	1.4	4	1.8
Falls	19	2.2	10	4.4
Fires	20	2.3	9	3.9
Lightning	5	0.6	3	1.3
Drowning	50	5.8	6	2.6
Respiratory Obstruction	12	1.4	6	2.6
Firearms (Unintentional)	2	0.2	0	—
Electric Current	1	0.1	1	0.4
Other/Late Effects	115	13.4	16	7.0
INTENTIONAL INJURY	165	19.2	28	12.2
Suicide (Total)	82	9.5	6	2.6
Drugs	0	—	3	1.3
Solid/Liquid	1	0.1	0	—
Hanging/Strangulation/ Suffocation	33	3.8	2	0.9
Handgun	5	0.6	0	—
Other/Unspec. Firearms	39	4.5	1	1.3
Other/Unspecified	4	0.5	0	—
Homicide (Total)	83	9.7	22	9.6
Assault (Total)	82	9.5	22	9.6
Firearms	12	1.4	6	2.6
Knife	37	4.3	3	1.3
Other/Late Effects	33	3.8	13	5.7
Legal Intervention	1	0.1	0	—
UNDETERMINED INTENTIONAL/ UNINTENTIONAL	24	2.8	7	3.1
TOTAL	861	100.1	229	100.0

Kunitz, 1971; May & Broudy, 1980; Broudy & May, 1983; Kunitz, 1983; Van Winkle & May, 1986). This follows the general pattern of rising suicide rates in the entire U.S., but rate for Navajos have risen more sharply (Van Winkle & May, 1986).

Van Winkle and May (1986) studied suicide in New Mexico Indians for the 22 year period from 1957 to 1979. During the 1960s, rates for Navajos ranged from 4 to 8 deaths per 100,000 for both sexes. By the end of the study period, rates had more than doubled. Navajo rates were generally lower than suicide rates of the Pueblo and Apache groups of New Mexico, approximately half that of the Pueblo and one-third of the Apache rate. However, the Navajo had the highest percent increase in rates over the time period, possibly as a result of an increase in suicides in the older (over 55) age groups. Suicide in these age groups was uncommon in the time period 1957–1968, but increased dramatically in the 1969–1979 period.

Suicide is currently the eighth leading cause of death among Navajo males with an age adjusted rate of 31.0 per 100,000, compared to 19.9 for U.S. white males in 1985 and 11.3 for U.S. black males (NCHS, 1989). Suicide is predominantly a male phenomenon, especially among the Navajo. There were 14 times more male than female suicides in the four years of data included in this analysis. The age-adjusted mortality rate for Navajo women was only 1.7 per 100,000 population. For this reason, further data on Navajo female suicides will not be presented.

Figure 61 shows the age specific suicide rates for males. Navajo males have the highest rates of suicide in each age group from 25 through 64. The Navajo age pattern resembles that of black suicides, but at a much higher level. The U.S. white pattern is interesting. There is a steep rise in suicides at adolescence and early adulthood. Afterward the rate levels off until age 45 when it begins to rise; after age 75, it rises

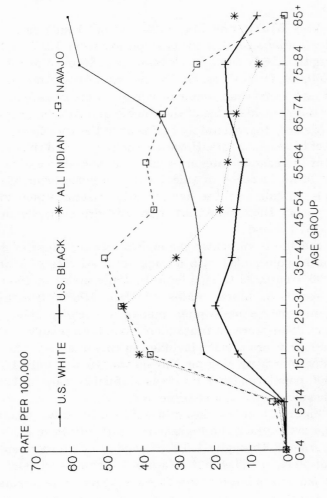

FIGURE 61
Male Suicide Mortality
Age Specific Rates

RATE PER 100,000

— U.S. WHITE   + U.S. BLACK   * ALL INDIAN   -□- NAVAJO

AGE GROUP

70
60
50
40
30
20
10

0-4   5-14   15-24   25-34   35-44   45-54   55-64   65-74   75-84   85+

U.S. DATA, 1985;SOURCE: NCHS
INDIAN DATA 1983-86 AVG.

again sharply. Rates for the other comparison groups have either dropped off sharply or are relatively low.

Using previous research on Navajo suicides (Levy, 1964; Van Winkle & May, 1986), Figure 62 shows the age specific rates for four time periods. The rates are highest in early adulthood for the 1969–1979 time period. The current data seems to be more similar to earlier times for these age groups up to age 54. At the older age groups, however, a curious trend appears to emerge. Increasingly, older Navajo males are committing suicide. During the 1970s, suicides were occurring in a decade of age (65–74) where no suicides were observed previously. In the 1980s data, we see this pattern extended to the 75–84 age group.

Navajo males choose extremely lethal methods of committing suicide (Figure 63). Firearms predominate (54%), followed by hanging, strangulation or suffocation (40%). These two methods comprise 93% of male suicides. Handguns account for a very small proportion of the firearms category; the hunting rifle is a much more common possession on the reservation.

Van Winkle and May (1983) report another interesting observation about Navajo suicides. Most males were married (54%), in contrast to the Apache (21%) and Pueblo (38%) suicides. This same pattern was observed by Levy (1965) as well.

Dizmang, et al. (1974) assert that the reservation system has made the male role obsolete, and that the man's status within the family structure has diminished, resulting in the "matrix for the present social and cultural chaos." This is social disorganization theory at the exchange level, and in Durkheimian tradition, high suicide rates are attributed to chaotic social structure.

One of the significant findings of Dizmang's case-control study of young (<25 years) Shoshone suicides was the prevalence of more than one caretaker before age 15 among the suicide cases. Of all the suicides in this group, 70% had

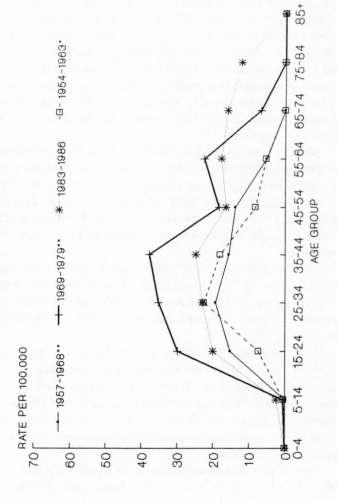

FIGURE 62
Age Specific Navajo Suicide Rates
Males, Four Time Periods

*Source: Levy, 1964
**Source: Van Winkle & May, 1986

FIGURE 63
Methods of Suicide
Indian Males

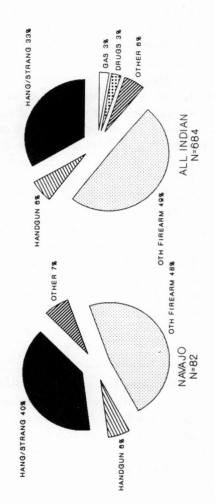

HANG/STRANG 33%

GAS 3%

DRUGS 3%

OTHER 6%

HANDGUN 6%

ALL INDIAN
N=684

OTH FIREARM 49%

OTHER 7%

OTH FIREARM 46%

NAVAJO
N=82

HANG/STRANG 40%

HANDGUN 6%

more than one caretaker, compared to 1% of controls, age- and sex-matched, and excluded and replaced if another suicide had occurred in the household.

Shoshone child-rearing custom was to use multiple caretakers in youth in an attempt to shelter the child from the physical and emotional trauma that could be expected from the early death of the mother, not an uncommon event when maternal mortality was quite high. In earlier times, these caretakers were well known to the child, part of his kinship system, and routinely seen by the child. The land division that occurred as part of the reservation formation disrupted the extended family and removed kin from the day to day life of children. However, the practice of placing children with kin for an extended time during times of hardship or at the birth of a new child did not change. Half the suicide cases in Dizmang's study experienced two or more losses by divorce or desertion, compared to 10% of the controls. These two reported statistics, undoubtedly correlated with each other, were each significant at the .005 level. This study is an example of the usefulness of exploring the role of cultural, perhaps ecologically evolved, practices for a greater understanding of some behaviors.

Homicide

Data presented in Chapter 5 revealed that homicide is in the five leading causes of death for Navajo males in every age group beyond infancy up to age 45. The age adjusted death rate for all ages is 28.1 per 100,000 population, compared to 8.1 for white males and 49.9 for black males (NCHS, 1989). Thus the Navajo rate is triple that of white males, but only half that of black males.

The age-specific mortality rates from homicide (Figure 64) show a Navajo pattern similar to that of all Indians, but different from both blacks and whites. Part of the difference may be due to the effect of small numbers, but the differences are so striking that they should be mentioned. Male Navajo infants are at higher risk of being murdered than males of all ages combined. They are also at almost triple the risk of black male infants. From ages one through four, Navajos also lead all the comparison groups, and again in the 15–24 age category. The risk of being murdered is highest in young adulthood for all four groups. In black and white males, the rates decline sharply and then level off in the older age groups. But, both the Navajo and the all Indian group show increases at older ages; in the Navajo, rates are as high at ages 65–74 as they are between the ages of 15 and 34. The all Indian peak is the 75–84 age group, but it is well below the level of early adulthood.

Deaths from homicide are almost four times more common in Navajo males than in females. Almost half the Navajo male homicide deaths were from knife wounds (46%); 14% resulted from the use of firearms (Figure 65). Handguns were responsible for only 1.2% of the firearm deaths. In Navajo females, 27% of deaths resulted from firearms, and only 18% from knifing. However, a large proportion of homicide deaths were due to other means and late effects of assault. It is impossible to know, from these data, what type of weapon was used in the assaults. Legal interventions accounted for one percent of homicides in males; no females died from legal intervention.

In the all Indian group, firearms were the leading weapon (37%), followed closely by knives (36%). The proportion of other and late effects was much lower in the all Indian group than in the Navajo. On comparing homicide and suicide rates between ethnic groups, an interesting pattern emerges. Navajo males have identical rates of homicide and suicide. In U.S. white males, the suicide rate is more than double that of the homicide rate; in U.S. blacks the homicide rate is more than quadruple that of the suicide rate (NCHS, 1985:47). The pattern in black and white females is the same at much lower levels, but in Navajo women homicide is almost

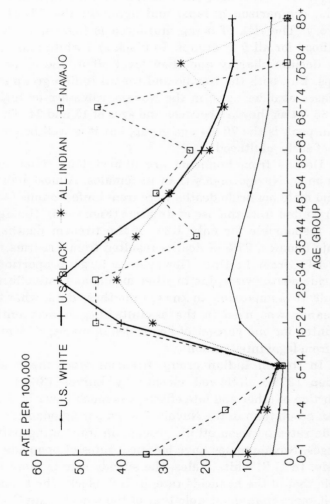

FIGURE 64
Male Homicide Mortality
Age Specific Rates

RATE PER 100,000

U.S. WHITE   U.S. BLACK   ALL INDIAN   NAVAJO

AGE GROUP

U.S. DATA, 1985; SOURCE: NCHS
INDIAN DATA 1983-86 AVG.

FIGURE 65

Methods of Homicide
Indian Males

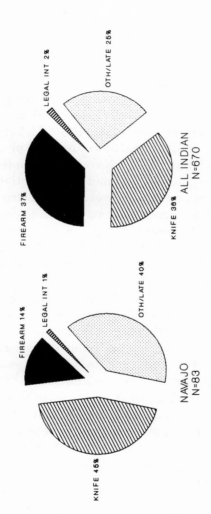

HANDGUN = 1.2% NAVAJO, 2.1% ALL INDIAN

four times more common than suicide. Only six cases of Navajo female suicide were recorded between 1983 and 1986.

Alcoholism

A detailed discussion of the patterns of drinking and the health effects of alcohol among American Indians is beyond the scope of this investigation. However, there are a number of studies which focus exclusively on alcohol and Native Americans (MacAndrew & Edgerton, 1969; Mohatt, 1972; May, 1977; Waddell & Everett, 1980). Alcohol precipitated morbidity and mortality among the Navajo are complicated by a number of factors, including myth and misconception.

Unbeknownst to many, the prevalence of drinking in this population is less common than in the general U.S. population (May 1982). Another common misconception is that Indians metabolize alcohol differently, predisposing them to more adverse effects (May, 1982). Navajos themselves believe this myth (Smith, 1984).

The U.S. policy toward alcohol and American Indians, in history, has been one of ambivalence. Alcohol was first introduced to native populations as a means of establishing friendship; later it had become a profitable trade commodity, and it was even used to deceive and swindle Indians of their possessions, including land. Congress outlawed the liquor trade with Indians in 1832 under the auspices of trustees, and in defiance of tribal sovereignty. However, since 1953, laws regulating the sale and use of alcohol on the reservation have been under the jurisdiction of the tribes themselves (May, 1976). The Navajo have chosen, partly out of denial, to retain the earlier government-imposed prohibition laws.

The problem, as I see it, is that Indians in general were socialized into drinking patterns by frontiersmen and miners whose own drinking behavior was aberrant. These drinking patterns became integrated into cultural practices, and have been reinforced by conditions of high unemployment, low status attainment potential, and by prohibition itself. Prohibition is associated with binge drinking, and emphasizes rapid consumption and intoxication (May, 1976).

Factors in addition to those already mentioned that cloud our understanding of alcohol problems among Indians include the age distribution of the population and reporting differences between Indian and other population groups. Young people are more likely to use alcohol than older individuals. Because of high fertility, a greater proportion of the Navajo population is young, and at higher risk for alcohol experimentation (May, 1989). Secondly, public awareness focused upon the alcohol problems of Indians makes it more likely that deaths attributable to alcohol will be recorded as such, in comparison to the general population.

Tables 43 and 44 show the numbers of deaths attributed to alcoholism in each of the three cause categories by sex and age, and the age-specific death rates for all causes combined. Male rates are more than double the rates for females in all age groups, but they are more than triple in the over 65 year age group. The highest rates of alcoholism deaths are observed in the 35–44 age group for both sexes.

TABLE 43

Alcoholism Deaths by Cause of Death, Age Group, and Age
Specific Alcoholism Death Rates/100,000
Navajo Area Male Deaths, 1983–1986

Age Group	Alcoholic Psychosis	Alcohol Dependency Syndrome	Alcoholic Cirrhosis	Total Age Specific Rate
15–24	0	1	1	3.27
25–34	0	18	15	99.83
35–44	1	15	15	121.75
45–64	3	13	14	95.11
65 +	0	4	3	50.75
All Ages	4	51	48	32.56

TABLE 44

Alcoholism Deaths by Cause of Death, Age Group, and Age
Specific Alcoholism Death Rates/100,000
Navajo Area Female Deaths, 1983–1986

Age Group	Alcoholic Psychosis	Alcohol Dependency Syndrome	Alcoholic Cirrhosis	Total Age Specific Rate
15–24	0	1	0	1.47
25–34	0	7	7	35.66
35–44	0	5	11	51.75
45–64	0	4	12	45.99
65 +	0	0	2	14.92
All Ages	0	17	32	14.51

Cancer

Age-adjusted cancer mortality rates among the Navajo
population are half the U.S. white rates for males and three-
fourths the rate for females. Crude death rates are even lower
due to the youthfulness of the Navajo population. If cancer
were eliminated as a cause of death, it would add less than a
year to the life expectancy of working age Navajos (see
Chapter 5).

Malignant neoplasms account for approximately 8% of
Navajo male and 16% of female deaths. In contrast, 23% of
U.S. white male and 28.2% of white female deaths resulted
from malignant neoplasms (NCHS, 1988). The all Indian rates
are similar to those of the Navajo. The crude rate for females
is 56.6, compared to 60.3 for all Indian women and 175.1 for
all U.S. women (IHS, 1989; NCHS, 1985). For males, the rate
for Navajos is 52.2, compared to 69.1 for all Indians and 212.6
for all U.S. males.

In Navajo females the three leading cancer sites are
breast, gallbladder, and stomach (Table 45). For U.S. females

TABLE 45

Percent Distribution of Cancer Deaths by Site and Sex
Navajo Area Deaths, 1983–1986

Cancer Site	Male #	Male %	Female #	Female %
Lip, Oral Cavity, Pharynx	3	1.8	1	0.5
Stomach	22	13.3	18	9.4
Colon & Rectum	6	3.6	4	2.1
Liver & Bile Ducts	6	3.6	10	5.2
Gallbladder	9	5.5	24	12.6
Pancreas	12	7.3	11	5.8
Trachea, Bronchus, Lung	20	12.1	6	3.1
Bone & Soft Tissue	7	4.2	4	2.1
Melanoma	2	1.2	2	1.0
Prostate & Testes	13	7.9	N/A	N/A
Breast	0	0.0	27	14.1
Cervix	N/A	N/A	16	8.4
Uterus	N/A	N/A	3	1.6
Ovary	N/A	N/A	9	4.7
Bladder & Kidney	9	5.5	7	3.7
Brain	4	2.4	3	1.6
Lymphatic & Hematopoietic	17	10.3.	10	5.2
Other & Unspecified	35	21.2	36	18.8
All Sites	165	99.9	191	99.9
Crude Death Rate		**52.2**		**56.6**
Age Adjusted Rate		**78.4**		**84.6**

the leading sites are lung, breast, and colorectal cancers (SEER, 1984). For Navajo males, stomach, lung, and male genital cancers are the leading causes of cancer deaths. Lung, colorectal and male genital cancers lead the list for U.S. males (SEER, 1984). The two sites of cancer that are more common in Navajos are stomach and gallbladder, while colorectal cancer is less common than in the general U.S. population.

Figures 66 and 67 show the age specific cancer rates of Navajo males and females, compared to all Indians and U.S. whites and blacks. Both sexes follow the same age pattern as the comparison groups.

Gallbladder cancer is elevated in Navajo females, as has been documented in a classic study of cancer mortality in American Indians from 1950 to 1967 (Creagan & Fraumeni, 1972). In fact, gallbladder cancer was the only site which was significantly higher in Indians than in U.S. whites and blacks.

Smoking is not prevalent among Navajos, which probably accounts for a low rate of many types of cancer. Stomach cancer has declined dramatically in Western industrialized countries, possibly attributable to widespread refrigeration of foods and dietary changes.

For the present, cancer cannot be said to be much of a problem on the Navajo reservation; its significance pales in comparison to accidental deaths. However, Samet, et al. (1987) found that American Indians in New Mexico and Arizona had poorer cancer survival rates than Anglo and Hispanic patients. They tended to present with more advanced lesions, and were not as likely to receive treatment. Even after adjusting for stage and treatment, however, Indians had poorer survival. Thus, cancer mortality might be reduced if cancers were diagnosed and treated earlier.

One additional caution is necessary at this point. The prevalence of smoking and other tobacco use should be closely monitored on the Navajo reservation. Changes in the prevalence of tobacco use will portend changes in cancer rates.

FIGURE 66
Male Cancer Mortality
Age Specific Rates

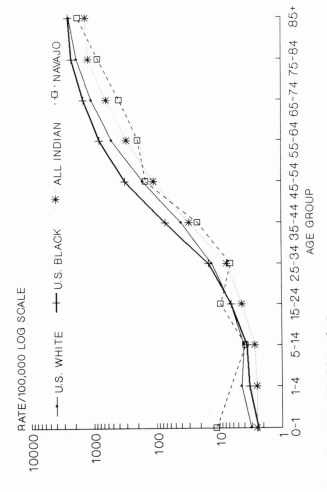

RATE/100,000 LOG SCALE

— U.S. WHITE   —+— U.S. BLACK   —*— ALL INDIAN   -□- NAVAJO

AGE GROUP

U.S. DATA, 1985; SOURCE: NCHS
INDIAN DATA 1983-86 AVG.

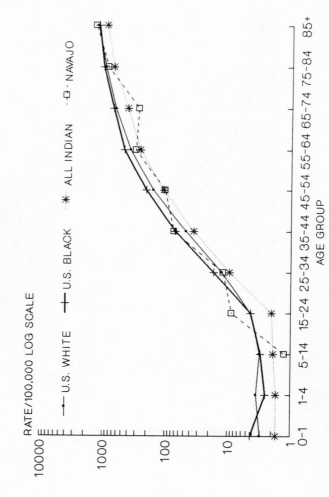

FIGURE 67
Female Cancer Mortality
Age Specific Rates

RATE/100,000 LOG SCALE

—•— U.S. WHITE   —|— U.S. BLACK   —*— ALL INDIAN   -□- NAVAJO

10000
1000
100
10
1

0-1   1-4   5-14   15-24   25-34   35-44   45-54   55-64   65-74   75-84   85+

AGE GROUP

U.S. DATA, 1985; SOURCE: NCHS
INDIAN DATA 1983-86 AVG.

Diabetes

The 1985 age adjusted mortality rate from diabetes is three times higher in Navajo women (26.4/100,000) and more than twice as high in Navajo men (22.0/100,000), compared to U.S. white males (9.2/100,000) and females (8.0/100,000) (NCHS, 1988). The rate for all Indians is also high: 13.6 for males and 18.2 for females. Figures 68 and 69 show the age specific rates for diabetes by sex.

Increased prevalence and mortality of diabetes in American Indians has been well publicized and linked to rapid Westernization, obesity, fat distribution, and genetic susceptibility (Gardner, et al., 1984). One hypothesis is that certain genetically susceptible populations, such as the American Indian, are predisposed to obesity and diabetes under Western conditions of plentiful food (Neel, 1962). This genetic predisposition would have been to their survival advantage under conditions of scarcity, according to the hypothesis. Studies of a number of Amerindian groups, most notably the Pima, have shown that diabetes was rare prior to 1940, but now the prevalence rate approaches 40% in Pimas 35 and older (Cowen, 1990). Additional support for the genetic hypothesis has been provided by studies of Hispanics, whose heritage includes admixture with American Indians, and whose rates are intermediate between those of U.S. whites and Indians (Hanis, et al., 1983; Samet, et al., 1988). African Americans are not at increased risk for mortality from diabetes (NCHS, 1988).

Prevention of diabetes and reduction of mortality among the Navajo may rest on improved screening and management of diagnosed cases, combined with radical and long-term changes in diet and exercise of high risk individuals.

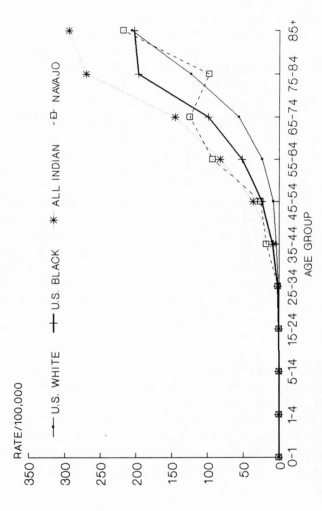

FIGURE 68
Male Diabetes Mortality
Age Specific Rates

RATE/100,000

— U.S. WHITE ⊹ U.S. BLACK ✳ ALL INDIAN ⊡ NAVAJO

350
300
250
200
150
100
50
0

0-1 1-4 5-14 15-24 25-34 35-44 45-54 55-64 65-74 75-84 85+

AGE GROUP

U.S. DATA, 1985; SOURCE: NCHS
INDIAN DATA 1983-86 AVG.

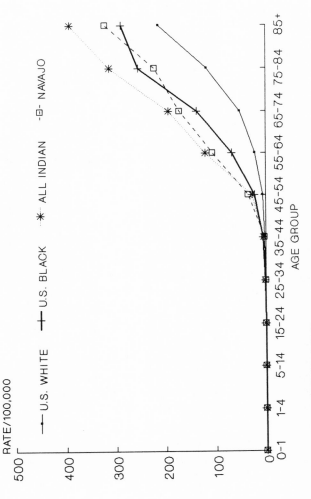

FIGURE 69
Female Diabetes Mortality
Age Specific Rates

─┼─ U.S. WHITE   ─┼─ U.S. BLACK   ─*─ ALL INDIAN   ─▫─ NAVAJO

RATE/100,000

500

400

300

200

100

0

0-1 1-4 5-14 15-24 25-34 35-44 45-54 55-64 65-74 75-84 85+

AGE GROUP

U.S. DATA, 1985; SOURCE: NCHS
ALL INDIAN DATA 1984-86 AVG.

Pneumonia and Influenza

Pneumonia and influenza mortality rates are slightly higher in Navajo males than for U.S. males. The age adjusted rates are 34.0/100,000 for Navajos and 28.5/100,000 for U.S. males (NCHS, 1988). However, the rate for females is lower (18.9) than the U.S. rate (28.1).

Figures 70 and 71 show the age and sex specific rates for Navajos and the comparison groups. Generally, Navajos are at increased risk of death from pneumonia and influenza only in the earliest and latest years of life. U.S. whites have the lowest rates of pneumonia and influenza, except their rates exceed those of blacks in the age category 85 and older.

Kunitz (1983) reports much higher rates of pneumonia and influenza in earlier years. From 1954 to 1956, the mortality rates ranged from 99 to 114 per 100,000 population, excluding newborns. In the 1960s (1965–1967), the rates were approximately halved to 53–61 per 100,000. By the time period 1973–1975, rates had declined further, but not as steeply as earlier, to 35–41 deaths per 100,000. Thus we can see continued improvement in the treatment, and perhaps resistance, to pneumonia and influenza. It is the last remaining infectious disease among the leading causes of death in Navajos of all ages.

Pneumonia and influenza deaths overshadow all other causes of respiratory disease mortality. There were many more cases of pneumonia and influenza than any other cause of death in this grouping (Table 46). For example, there were 138 cases of pneumonia and influenza in this time period, but only 29 cases of tuberculosis, 25 cases of lung cancer, and 22 cases of chronic obstructive pulmonary disease. The category with the second largest number of cases was the other respiratory category (ICD 510–519). Some of the deaths coded to this cause might be deaths that should have been coded elsewhere, or would have been if more information had been available.

TABLE 46

Respiratory Disease Mortality by Cause and Sex
Navajo Area Deaths, 1983–1986

Cause of Death (ICD)	Male		Female	
	#	%	#	%
Tuberculosis (ICD 10-18, 137)	14	7.1	15	14.2
Pneumonia & Influenza (ICD 470-478, 480-487)	88	44.7	50	47.2
Cancer of Lung (ICD 162)	20	10.2	5	4.7
Cancer of Larynx (ICD 161)	0	—	1	0.9
Other Respiratory Cancer (ICD 160, 163-165)	2	1.0	1	0.9
COPD* (ICD 491, 492, 496)	22	11.1	0	—
Asthma (ICD 493)	4	2.0	0	—
Bronchiectasis (ICD 494-495)	2	1.0	7	6.6
Pneumoconiosis (ICD 500-508)	13	6.6	7	6.6
Other (ICD 510–519, 460- 466)	32	16.2	20	18.9
Total	197	99.9	106	100.0

Symptoms, Signs, and Ill-Defined Causes

This "catch-all" category of death includes such statements by certifiers as senility, natural causes, unattended death, and found dead. It is important to examine rates of ill-defined deaths because deaths coded to this category may actually belong in other specific causes of death. High rates of ill-defined deaths may introduce bias into studies of mortality by cause of death.

Ill-defined causes of death are three times higher in Navajo males than in all U.S. males, and they are more than double in Navajo females compared to U.S. females. The age adjusted rates are 48.9 and 24.7 per 100,000 for Navajo males and females, respectively. For the entire U.S., the rates are 15 for males and 11 for females (NCHS, 1988).

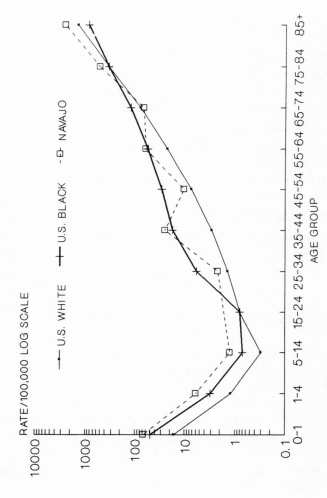

FIGURE 70

Male Pneumonia & Influenza Mortality
Age Specific Rates

RATE/100,000 LOG SCALE

— U.S. WHITE   —┼— U.S. BLACK   -☐- NAVAJO

AGE GROUP

0-1 1-4 5-14 15-24 25-34 35-44 45-54 55-64 65-74 75-84 85+

10000 1000 100 10 1 0.1

U.S. DATA, 1985; SOURCE: NCHS
INDIAN DATA 1983-86 AVG.

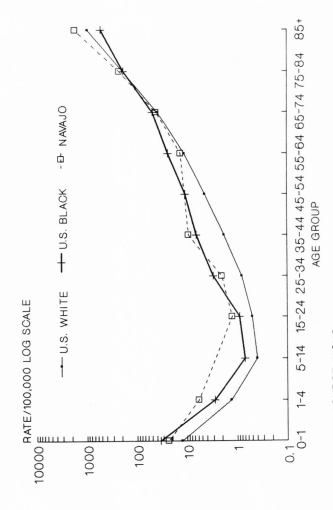

FIGURE 71
Female Pneumonia & Influenza Mortality
Age Specific Rates

RATE/100,000 LOG SCALE

— U.S. WHITE   —+— U.S. BLACK   -□- NAVAJO

AGE GROUP

0-1 1-4 5-14 15-24 25-34 35-44 45-54 55-64 65-74 75-84 85+

U.S. DATA, 1985; SOURCE: NCHS
INDIAN DATA 1983-86 AVG.

Looking at Figures 72 and 73, we can see the excess is primarily in the older (over age 55) age groups, but that males aged 1–14 and females aged 5–14 are also at increased risk of dying from ill-defined causes. U.S. whites have the lowest risk at all ages.

Becker, et al. (1990) studied New Mexico death certificates from 1958 to 1982 and found that both American Indian and Hispanic rates of death from non-specific ICD codes were higher than for non-Hispanic whites. However, rates in the time period 1978–1982 for all three ethnic groups studied exceeded those of U.S. whites and U.S. blacks. In fact, Becker's reported age adjusted rates for New Mexico American Indians (standardized to the 1970 U.S. population) are more than double the Navajo rates in 1983–1986.

There are at least three possible explanations for the puzzling inconsistency in rates. First, the use of different standard populations for age adjustment may account for the difference. Second, there may be significant differences between Navajos and other New Mexico Indians, although this is unlikely. Third, it is possible that coding changes from ICD-8 to ICD-9, which occurred during Becker's study period, or changes in death certification occurred. Further investigation is needed to account for the observed differences in rates in a short period of time.

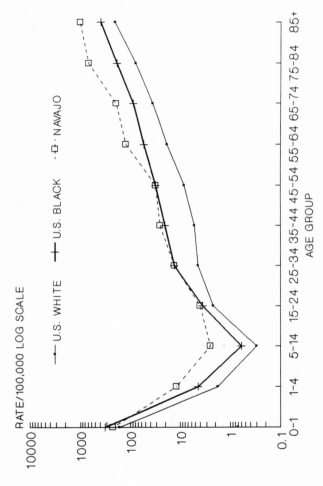

FIGURE 72
Male Ill-Defined Mortality
Age Specific Rates

RATE/100,000 LOG SCALE

— U.S. WHITE — U.S. BLACK - □ - NAVAJO

AGE GROUP

0-1 1-4 5-14 15-24 25-34 35-44 45-54 55-64 65-74 75-84 85+

10000
1000
100
10
1
0.1

U.S. DATA, 1985; SOURCE: NCHS
INDIAN DATA 1983-86 AVG.

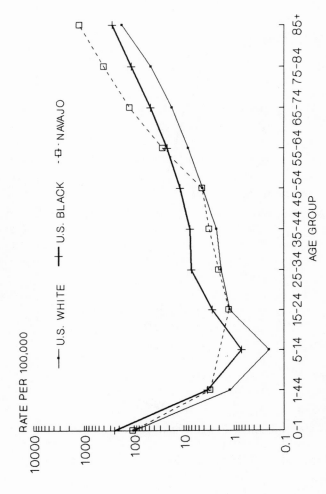

FIGURE 73
Female Ill-Defined Mortality
Age Specific Rates

U.S. DATA, 1985; SOURCE: NCHS
INDIAN DATA 1983-86 AVG.

Chapter **8**

DISCUSSION

We have seen that levels and patterns of Navajo fertility and mortality differ from the U.S. pattern in important ways. These patterns have been shaped by past and present environmental and social circumstances, and by the perceptions and choices made by individuals affected by these circumstances. Demographic patterns, in turn, shape the future environmental and social reality of the Navajo. Thus the demographic variables of fertility, mortality, and migration may be viewed as both a cause and a consequence of Navajo social structure. As a result of data limitations, this research has focused on fertility and mortality to the almost total exclusion of migration except as a dependent variable, with a only a hint of its potential importance as a causal or independent variable. In this chapter some of the implications of migration as an important demographic variable will be discussed.

The three key demographic variables, then, are inextricably bound together in the effects that they produce and that are produced by them. One of the key findings of this research has been the importance of culture in shaping demographic patterns. When poor environmental conditions were the overarching cause of mortality, cultural contributions were obscured. It was easy, and probably appropriate, to attribute high mortality to poverty and to environmental conditions. High fertility under these conditions was easily explained as a result of high mortality. However, as mortality has declined, in conjunction with sanitary improvements and the availability of medical care, the impact of culture has become more visible. High fertility can no longer be explained as a response to high mortality.

However, some demographic patterns among the Navajo are unexpectedly similar to those of the U.S., especially considering the wide socioeconomic disparity that exists. The most notable differences are found in infant mortality rates and female life expectancy.

We may need to rethink our well-established, but perhaps erroneous, beliefs about the connection between socioeconomic status and demographic patterns. There appear to be other possibilities apart from, or in conjunction with, economic well-being that affect patterns of fertility and mortality. That Navajo women enjoy virtually the same expectation of life and the same favorable birth outcomes as the vastly more privileged group of white women is inconceivable, given our belief in the "advantage of advantage." These findings suggest we must redirect our inquiries into the determinants of fertility and mortality patterns.

In this concluding chapter, I shall attempt to summarize and interpret these similarities and differences, and point to areas where future research would seem to be most productive. Theoretical dimensions outlined in Chapter 2 will be discussed in light of the data presented.

The findings of this investigation raise a number of questions . . . more questions, in fact, than answers. First, while Navajo fertility has declined, it remains quite high in spite of the fact that infant mortality is virtually the same as for the U.S., and age-adjusted mortality from all causes combined is only slightly higher. This situation has resulted in exceedingly high rates of natural increase, which sets the stage for continued explosive growth of the population. Low sex ratios at birth and improved survival of females compared to males further enhances future growth potential. At current levels of fertility and mortality, the population can be expected to double in less than thirty years. The present land base cannot sustain even the current population, much less this magnitude of increase, with the land use policies in effect. The region remains agrarian and undeveloped.

The only realistic way of expanding the land base is through tribal purchase of private property. As we saw in Chapter 1, the Navajo Nation has spent millions of dollars in recent years pursuing this strategy. Dollars spent in acquiring new land mean fewer dollars are available for economic development . . . and only a development miracle could provide the resources necessary to support this rapidly growing population. Development in a haphazard or boom/bust pattern, as has occurred in the past, would not be productive.

Migration Pressures

Navajos are free to migrate from the reservation, but relatively few are inclined to do so. Eighty-two percent of the reservation population one year old and older have never lived off the reservation (Navajo Nation, 1988). Conversely, 1980 Census sample data reveal that 91% of Navajos counted in the census live in the three reservation states of Arizona, New Mexico and Utah (derived from Snipp, 1989). While not all live on reservation land per se, they are close enough to participate in tribal activities and maintain close ties with kin.

Traditional beliefs suggest that Navajos who venture out of the circle of protection of the four sacred mountains are in danger.

> When the population increases so much that the People spread out beyond the boundary represented by the God's body, that will be the end of the Navajos. Because Navajo people live beyond that boundary now, it could be that they will run into difficulties with nature and will be out of harmony with the plan of the Gods. (Yazzie, 1971:83)

Regardless of the prevailing attitudes toward migration, the pressure to migrate will intensify, especially for males who might have to rely on mothers, sisters, or wives for access to land, or on the availability of wage work on the reservation. Women will be reluctant to permanently migrate off the reservation for wage labor for a number of reasons. First, unless they are well educated, the jobs available to women do not pay well. Childcare and housing are real expenses off the reservation, whereas with an extended kinship network, these costs are minimal or free on the reservation. Entitlements may also be more difficult to obtain off the reservation (Metcalf, 1982).

Away from the protection of her kin, a woman might be more susceptible to neglect or abuse from a sexual partner, especially if alcohol is involved. Finally, there is the companionship of close relatives and the stress of an alien environment to consider. Perhaps the stress generated by social inequality and discrimination is less damaging on the reservation than off.

Conte's (1982) case study of the Begay sisters outlines a strategy of female networking and pooling of resources, combined with utilizing the resources of off-reservation kin (husbands, brothers and sons) for economic and political power. Between the three women, there were 22 offspring, and they formed a powerful political bloc in their area of the reservation.

The marginality of land and resources also make sending some kin off-reservation a desirable strategy for remittances and weekend or holiday assistance. Stark (1981) has suggested that adult migrant children, especially educated ones, can provide valuable "financial intermediary" services to rural households wishing to modernize. Some of the services provided by these migrants include capital formation, risk reduction, and expertise in the urban setting. This expertise might include legal, financial, and social knowledge beyond the scope of the rural residents. With this

line of reasoning, Stark postulates that the demand for
children to fulfill different roles might actually increase or
keep high the demand for children during economic
development, or the transition from a household-based to a
capitalist mode of production. In Stark's words, children can
be a source of:

> several different benefits. But not all children—or any
> particular child—can efficiently provide all utilities,
> especially in a less developed economy. Specialization by
> children in the production of different utilities increases
> total utility from children; and specialization and
> indivisibility often imply that the same child cannot provide
> "supply side" competing utilities. . . . Finally, a high degree
> of specialization by children in the provision of different
> utilities sharply reduces the possibility of cross-substitution
> among children; this, in turn, increases the risk involved in
> losing a particular child. In these circumstances, the
> number of children becomes crucial to the risk-averse
> household. This once again favors a high level of fertility.
> (Stark, 1981:674)

Extant High Fertility

It appears that the social organization of the Navajo
relates directly to the level of fertility and the pattern of
mortality through established gender roles. Matrilineal
descent, residence, and inheritance encourages high fertility
in at least two ways: by lowering the costs of having children
through kin-provided child care, and by exacerbating fragile
spousal relations, thereby making high fertility desirable for
old age security.

The Navajo culture of reciprocity, ecologically based in
long-term scarcity or unpredictability of resources (Baker &
Sanders, 1972), also encourages high fertility. Enough
offspring of both sexes are needed to ensure an adequate pool
for both day-to-day duties and the demands of reciprocity.

Historically, high fertility has had attendant health consequences for women. From 1915 until the mid-1930s, maternal mortality in the U.S. ranged from six to eight maternal deaths per **1,000** live births (Census Bureau, 1952). In 1986, the maternal mortality rate in the U.S. was seven deaths per **100,000** live births, a dramatic decline (NCHS, 1989). Improved nutrition, standards of living, and access to and utilization of medical care have contributed to this decline. Navajo women appear to be experiencing few adverse effects of high fertility. Both maternal and infant mortality rates are surprisingly low.

Maternal mortality rates could be slightly affected by intermarriage patterns. Non-Indian women carrying a Navajo baby would not be included in the numerator if they died in childbirth.

As mentioned in Chapter 1, early differences in growth rates between the Navajo and Hopi resulted from differences in mortality, specifically, improved survival of Navajo offspring. However, more recent growth rate differentials can be attributed to fertility. Kunitz and Slocumb (1975) demonstrate that while Hopi women have fewer induced abortions, they have more hysterectomies and bilateral tubal ligations performed during the childbearing years. However, Hopi women have more induced abortions than Navajo women above the age of 40, indicating greater utilization of surgical procedures for fertility control. As would be expected, Hopi women have lower age specific fertility rates in the older age groups.

We must also ask whether aspects of Navajo childbearing that appear to be similar to the pattern in African Americans do, in fact, stem from the same causal mechanisms. The most striking similarities between the two groups are the high rates of single and early childbearing. In blacks, early childbearing may be an adaptive strategy, a hedge against the deleterious effects of malnutrition, venereal disease, and blocked opportunities. African American women have, on average, less than half a child more than white women, but Navajo women have two additional children compared to whites. Black women curtail their fertility in older childbearing age groups; Navajo women do not. Fertility continues to be elevated until the end of the childbearing years.

It does not appear that the steady decline in infant mortality rates has reduced the number of "insurance babies" appreciably. But even the oldest mothers of the population studied report fairly low childhood mortality experiences. Over the past 20 years, Navajo birthrates have declined slightly, but large reductions in infant mortality have been achieved.

Usually, women are forced to choose between quantity and quality of offspring, with costs attending either choice. For example, if child survival is low and the cost of placing children on the marriage market is unattainable, then women might choose to have many children, knowing that some may die and hoping that some will eventually succeed. Alternatively, when child survival is high and a woman has access to resources to educate and place a few children in positions to succeed in life, then that woman may limit her fertility to those whom she has the resources to help educate, marry, and reproduce.

For Navajo women, the costs of placing children on the marriage market do not appear to be a major consideration. But child survival (at least infant survival), the other component of quality, is high. Thus, the apparent low cost of combining strategies has not forced Navajo women to choose between quantity and quality of children.

Rates of single childbearing in the Navajo bear questioning as well. The rates are extremely high (75%) for first births, and decline steadily thereafter, more so than in blacks. As Lamphere (1974) has noted, Navajo marriage becomes more stable over time.

The conditions predictive of high rates of single parenthood cited by Lancaster (1989) are certainly present in the Navajo. On the other hand, trends in the general U.S. population show a fourfold increase in rates of single childbearing since 1960, and a sixfold increase has occurred in whites (NCHS, 1985). In the U.S., over one in five children are born to unmarried mothers; one in seven to whites.

The tendency of whites to converge with the higher rates of ethnic minorities suggests that a pervasive change is taking place throughout the United States. From among the perspectives mentioned in Chapter 2, only the biosocial perspective and the sex ratio theory of Guttentag and Secord (1983) could have predicted these trends. Both portend far-reaching changes in family life for perhaps a majority of the population.

Minority Group Status and Fertility

Is the observed high fertility among the Navajo a result of minority group status? Several studies have focused on the relationship between minority group status and high fertility (Goldscheider & Uhlenberg, 1969; Sly, 1970; Kennedy, 1973; Roberts & Lee, 1974; Stephen, 1987). Two competing hypotheses have arisen to explain high fertility in minorities: 1) that minority group status exerts an independent effect on fertility; and 2) that when socioeconomic variables are controlled, minority status exerts no independent effect. The second hypothesis would predict that, as minorities become assimilated, their fertility levels converge with the majority.

Roberts and Lee (1974) have pointed out several methodologic weaknesses in the Sly (1970) and Goldscheider and Uhlenberg (1969) studies. First, cumulative rather than current fertility measures were used, obscuring possible effects of assimilation in the younger population. Second, Sly (1970) examined only black/white fertility differentials, and Goldscheider and Uhlenberg compared five groups, mixing race, national origin, and religion as indicators of minority group status. Black/white and white/non-white classifications of data have dominated social and epidemiologic studies until recently, as the need to collect and present data for Hispanics has become documented. Researchers in the Southwest have been particularly hampered by both the dearth and inconsistency of data for Hispanic and American Indian populations.

Hispanics have been traditionally mixed with the "white" population until the 1980 census. Now some census data are available for them as a separate group, and in other data, they are spread among the racial categories "black," "white" and "other." Indians traditionally fall into the "other" or "non-white" categories, and comprise only a small percentage of each group. Pueblo Indians in the Southwest may be included in Hispanic statistics if surname is used as the ethnic identifier, since many have Spanish surnames.

As we have seen, the pattern of low birth weight childbearing in Indians no more resembles the pattern in blacks than does the lung cancer experience in Hispanics resemble that of non-Hispanic whites (Samet, et al., 1980). Roberts and Lee (1974) make a convincing case for separating the Spanish surname population from whites when examining fertility patterns. Using 1970 census data, they found increased support for the independent effects of minority group status hypothesis by doing so. At the very least, they suggest that structural (education, SES) and cultural (values and norms) components of assimilation must be considered separately. Unfortunately, cultural aspects of acculturation are available only when collected by special surveys, concepts may be operationalized differently by different researchers, and the salient questions may vary among minority groups.

Stephen's (1987) study of fertility among Navajos presented in Chapter 2 found differences in fertility, even after socioeconomic status was controlled. She also points out that unlike other minorities, American Indians are not an immigrant group. Many of the ways in which assimilation factors have been operationalized are specific to immigrant groups, and not relevant to American Indians, nor to some Hispanics.

Yinger (1985) has proposed that assimilation is a multidimensional and bidirectional process. The subprocesses of assimilation may occur at varying rates and include changes at the psychological, cultural, structural, and biologic levels. Many researchers have used the terms assimilation and acculturation interchangeably, or have assumed that variables operationalized on one dimension can effectively serve as a proxy for the entire process.

Yinger (1985) and Metcalf (1982) have also pointed out that acculturation may erroneously be viewed as substitutive, that is, one culture is gradually replaced by another. Metcalf identified four distinct types of urban Navajo women. In addition to the traditional and acculturated, she found a bi-cultural group, and a "marginal" group detached from both cultures. Moreover, in Metcalf's sample, the degree of success women had attained in "white" society (occupation, education, residence) was positively correlated with the retention of Navajo behaviors. This finding suggests that it may be those who are more strongly attached to their native cultures adapt best to new cultural settings.

Further investigations of minority group status and fertility will have to resolve some of these methodologic issues, and pay careful attention to the concept and specification of ethnicity and assimilation variables.

It might also be relevant to note how much additional power has, in fact, accrued to the Navajo tribe as a result of their increased numbers. If the Navajo and other Indian groups are purposely pursuing a high fertility strategy for greater political leverage, it would not be without historical precedent (Stucki, 1971).

Gender Roles

The relative survival disadvantage of males in the young adult years stems from a pattern of risk-taking behaviors engaged in by young men: alcohol use, suicide, fighting, driving. These behaviors appear to result, in part, from cultural factors present in Navajo society.

They are also related to macrostructural conditions such as high unemployment. From a societal standpoint, young men seem to play no crucial role in reservation life, and are aware of it. Stable employment opportunities are scarce and may conflict with obligations owed to the mother's or sister's household.

Off-reservation life offers even fewer opportunities for success. A young Navajo male may be perceived as a full-fledged adult in an urban area off the reservation. But, his typical educational achievement, occupational skills, rural background, minority status, and deviant drinking behavior do not enhance his social desirability. The discrimination and limited opportunity structure for off-reservation Navajo males may cause additional stress and reinforce deviant behavior.

Reservation life that "enables" extended adolescence during a time in which Navajo men are seeking meaningful adulthood may seem, and may in fact be, the more benign of alternatives. If young men manage to survive the prolonged transition to socially acknowledged adult, they may be valued for their rarity.

Esteemed positions for reservation males include tribal officers and healers. These positions are usually filled by older men and may interfere with, or even preclude, participation in wage labor. In the case of healers, there is a long and virtually unpaid apprenticeship, and demand for these services is waning. In sum, there are few opportunities for the young Navajo male to achieve social standing either on or off the reservation.

The Navajo social organization also affects the relationships between men and women and children. Beginning with adolescence, males may become acutely aware that the traditional lifestyle provides them with little security, and it may or may not be accompanied by respect from a spouse or offspring. Women are plentiful (a result of past high mortality in males), and there may be little incentive for stable pair-bonding. The obligations owed to the family of birth do not cease with marriage, and it might easily seem that the addition of new responsibilities without perceivable benefits is rather pointless.

In terms of reproductive strategies of young Navajo males, many have little to offer their offspring, and it may appear that their contributions are not needed anyway. In such a case, these men may choose not to marry or invest in their children, but to pursue additional mating opportunities as a strategy for maximizing reproductive success.

High mortality among males is more accentuated in Navajos than in the general U.S. society, and is similar to the high mortality among African American males. Navajo women, on the other hand, appear to enjoy some protection from the deleterious consequences that befall minorities, perhaps, in part, because of the matrifocal social structure.

At the advent of puberty, Navajo religion celebrates the woman, but not the man. Changing Woman's first menstruation is culturally reenacted in the *Kinaalda*, a part of the Blessing Way ceremony. The *Kinaalda* "ushers the girl into society, invokes positive blessing on her, ensures her health, prosperity and well-being, and protects her from potential misfortunes" (Frisbie, 1967:9).

Shepardson (1982) provides additional evidence for the high status of women. Her data consist mainly of ethnographic reports, and pertain to three time periods: 1868 to 1933, 1933 to the early 1950s, and the 1980s. She concludes that Navajo women had high status that was temporarily eroded in the stock reduction period, and has been partially regained. It might be important to consider the effects of further development on the status of Navajo women; it is possible that development will erode their favorable status, as has happened in parts of Africa.

One of Shepardson's middle-aged informants made an especially insightful observation with regard to present gender roles:

> Things aren't better, they're just changing. We aren't trained for parenting. We were in boarding school and we didn't observe adults playing proper adult roles. Our men aren't disciplined for modern jobs. They haven't absorbed good values—either old or new. A lot of women are having trouble with their husbands. The only model the men have is the macho white man. They try to copy him and Navajo women object (Shepardson, 1982:163).

Another ethnographic report on the status of Navajo women living in Flagstaff suggest that they face additional stress by living off-reservation (Griffen, 1982). This study, done in the late 1970s, also emphasizes the role of the extended matrifocal family in providing and in times of need. The subjects in Griffen's study were twice as likely to both give to and receive aid from female relatives, compared to male relatives. Of the help they received from male relatives, equal proportions came from consanguine and affine relatives, but when women gave aid to male relatives, they were ten times more likely to give it to consanguine males than to affines.

Theoretical Shortcomings

Modernization theory, including demographic and epidemiologic transition theory, has one fatal flaw. Implicit in its assumptions is ever upward or forward movement, the unending march of progress. The potential negative side effects of progress are never mentioned, brushed aside, or simply inconceivable. Demographic transition theory, like other social theories, seeks equilibrium, homeostasis. Birth and death rates are high, low, or in the process of transition from high to low.

However, we are beginning to see worldwide evidence of some deleterious side effects of modernization. We must ask the hard question raised by Marvin Harris (1977): The gains have been real, but are they permanent? Infectious and parasitic diseases, once thought to be under control or in decline, are staging comebacks—antibiotic resistant tuberculosis and gonorrhea. Moreover, infectious and communicable diseases such as AIDS, Legionnaire's, and others, have emerged as specters to taunt our progress.

With the technological advances that have been achieved, it is easy to forget how powerless medicine really is in the face of chronic and indiscriminate assault on the environment, a mutant virus, or an antibiotic resistant strain of a common microorganism. AIDS may be a more modern cause of death than plague, but is it qualitatively different? The battle is and was one in which the enemy changes even as we name it; it is the enemy lurking in the bedroom, in the walls and floors of our homes, at the dinner table, in the mirror, our beloved car, the air we breathe and what we drink.

What the epidemiologic transition calls degenerative disease and separates from those that are "man-made" are, in reality, artificial distinctions. COPD, degenerative heart disease, cancers, and many others are all "man-made," not in the same way as accidents, homicide, and suicide, but "man-made" nevertheless. Many of the communicable diseases also fall into this category, sexually transmitted diseases for example. As it turns out, adults are just as much the architects of their deaths as their parents were the architects of their births.

Epidemiologic transition theory was a useful extension of demographic transition theory and an important contribution to our understanding of changes in mortality in developed and developing countries when it was introduced. However, it now appears that categories of death specified by the theory obscure more than illuminate the underlying processes of, and life style interactions with, patterns of mortality. The idea of looking at differential mortality by cause of death is still important, perhaps more so than ever, but a change in focus is needed.

The efforts of the Indian Health Service undoubtedly played a major role in reducing the overall death rate among the Navajo as well as cause-specific deaths. Chief among these include tuberculosis and other infectious diseases, and infant mortality. However, as we examine the data presented in this study, it would be useful to ponder the practicality of medicine, per se, in attenuating deaths from such conditions as accidents, suicide, homicide, and alcoholism, except by improvements in emergency medical services. Even if these improvements were substantial, they could do nothing to address the underlying causes of the events requiring emergency services. It is doubtful that health care, as we have known it, can provide effective leadership in further mortality reductions, when the leading causes of death are not, in fact, diseases.

Kunitz sees modern medicine as increasingly playing the role of:

> an acculturating agent, teaching people to define conditions that are largely psychosocial in origin and rooted in traditional patterns of ecological adaptation and social organization as diseases for which new modes of explanation, treatment, and behavior are necessary. (Kunitz, 1983:3–4)

Kunitz acknowledges that the health problems of the Navajo have become increasingly complex and resistant to medical intervention, and that short of "profound changes in Navajo life" (Kunitz, 1983:186), the present pattern of mortality is not likely to change. The present pattern of medical response will also have to undergo profound change.

Kunitz ends his study of the Navajo on two cautionary notes. One is that ideological preconceptions about the future success or failure of medicine in treating specific diseases or conditions are not likely to be useful. Another is that, as health care providers venture into some of the more ambiguous areas, such as accidents and alcoholism, there are likely to be mistakes, both in conceptualization and in treatment or prevention.

There are alternative ways of viewing behaviors like continued heavy drinking. They range from normal to deviant in sociological terms and pathological in psychological and medical terms. That the medical model has become dominant, and a disease—alcoholism—has been labeled may or may not prove useful in changing individual behavior. There seems to be no overwhelming evidence that the medical model has interceded with conclusive results in the general population, much less with respect to the Navajo.

Evidence to support or refute the internal colonialism perspective will not be definitive until real development occurs on the reservation. However, enough questions have been raised about this theory that I believe it is not the most productive line of inquiry.

Caldwell's theory of changing family dynamics and wealth flow has potential, but it is predicated on a preexisting patriarchal structure, and assumes that young men will be the first recipients of mass education benefits. The fact that more women than men are in higher education and employed in BIA and IHS occupations requiring advanced skills, and the fact that the Navajo tribe has more advanced legislation pertaining to the equality of women than the United States, suggests that Caldwell's theory may have more relevance to other Third World societies than to the Navajo.

Cultural lag theory has been applied to immigrant groups and African Americans. Its usefulness in explaining the present data is very limited. We have seen the problems which can result when assimilation or acculturation is viewed as a linear, unidirectional, unidimensional, and substitutive process.

In summary, the data presented here have been best explained by the biosocial, cultural perspective. As Coale (1973) and Freedman (1979) have suggested, regional and temporal variations in demographic transition may be better explained by culture than by the macrostructural influences implied in transition theory. Some elements of demographic and epidemiologic transition theory have also been useful, but serious questions remain unanswered by this perspective.

Directions for Future Research

Several pieces of information needed to untangle the web of interactions and causal directions of variables related to Navajo demographic patterns are missing. In this section, I will try to point out areas of investigation that would enhance our understanding of the Navajo, and perhaps other populations as well.

First, the role of the Indian Health Service in reducing mortality must be explored. Are the free services provided by the IHS the cause of favorable birth outcomes among Navajo women? Would African American women with access to similar care be at less risk of delivering low birth weight infants, and would the survival of those infants be more favorable?

The IHS role is particularly important in light of the fact that complex behavioral patterns, as opposed to single agent diseases, dominate the current morbidity and mortality picture. How prepared are physicians and other health care workers to address complex, culturally ingrained, high risk behaviors? The contribution of alcohol to Navajo mortality is particularly salient, and must be discussed forthrightly by Navajo tribal leaders in the social and political context within which these behaviors occur, as well as by health care workers who attempt to treat the repercussions of these behaviors.

Second, migration studies of Navajos within and outside the reservation are needed. They are critical to understanding whether birth or death rates change in response to relocation. Population pressures, in turn, are increasingly likely to motivate people to migrate. We need a better understanding of, not only the demographic concomitants of migration, but the social, economic, and cultural aspects as well, particularly with regard to gender.

Sociological and anthropological studies of gender roles constitute a third area of needed research. Why are men at such increased survival disadvantage compared to women? What gender-related factors prompt early and single childbearing and maintain high fertility? What practices characterize male parental investment patterns among Navajos, and how are these different from other male parental investment patterns?

A particularly needed comparison is one between the matrifocal Navajo and another large tribe, perhaps the Sioux, that is patrilineal. The health consequences of alcohol abuse have been well-documented in the Sioux, but I am not aware of fertility or infant mortality statistics for this group, or of studies that detail gender differences in mortality.

Fourth, a linked birth and death certificate study of infant, and possibly childhood, mortality is warranted. We need to know whether prenatal care and other maternal behaviors during pregnancy, and how birth outcomes themselves, affect mortality.

Finally, numerator and denominator issues need more attention. With regard to the numerator, the high rates of ill-defined causes of death point to death certificate and hospital chart reviews, and possibly intensive educational efforts aimed at certifiers. Denominator needs include census enumeration surveillance and post-enumeration evaluations, as well as better intercensal estimates by age, sex, and geographic location. Large differences within the reservation were observed in this research, but these findings must be viewed with caution until more sophisticated estimates of service unit populations by age and sex exist. Intra-reservation migratory movements may make estimates using the last census as a base meaningless.

SELECTED BIBLIOGRAPHY

Aberle, D.F.
1966   *The Peyote Religion Among the Navaho*. Aldine Publishing
          Company, Chicago, IL.

Adams, M.S.
1973   Birth Weight of North American Indians: A Correction
          and Amplification. *Human Biology* 45(3):351–357.

Andress, V.R.
1977   Ethnic/Racial Misidentification in Death: A Problem
          Which May Distort Suicide Statistics. *Forensic Science*
          9:179–183.

Archer, V.E.
1981   Discussion of Secondary Sex Ratio of First-Born Offspring
          of U.S. Uranium Miners. In: *Birth Defects in the Four
          Corners Area* (W.H. Wiese, ed.). Transcript of a meeting.
          University of New Mexico School of Medicine,
          Albuquerque, NM.

Baker, P.T. and W.T. Sanders
1975   Demographic Studies in Anthropology. *Anthropological
          Studies of Human Fertility* (B.A. Kaplan, ed.). Wayne
          State University Press, Detroit, MI, pp. 151–178.

Baker, S.P., B. O'Neill and R.S. Karpf
1984   *The Injury Fact Book*. Lexington Books, Lexington, MA.

Beaver, S.E.
1975   *Demographic Transition Theory Reinterpreted*. Lexington
          Books, Lexington, MA.

Becker, G.S. and H.G. Lewis
1974   Interaction Between Quantity and Quality of Children. In:
          Economics of the Family: Marriage, Children and Human

233

Capital (T.W. Schultz, ed.). University of Chicago Press, Chicago, IL, pp. 81–90.

Becker, T.M., C.L. Wiggins, C.R. Key, and J.M. Samet
1990   Symptoms, Signs, and Ill-Defined Conditions: A Leading Cause of Death among Minorities. *American Journal of Epidemiology* 131:664–668.

Berelson, B.
1978   Prospects and Programs for Fertility Reduction: What? Where? *Population and Development Review* 4:579–616.

Berry, R.J., J.W. Buehler, L.T. Strauss, *et al.*
1987   Birth Weight-Specific Infant Mortality Due to Congenital Anomalies, 1960 and 1980. *Public Health Reports* 102:171–181.

Bianchi, S.
1990   America's Children: Mixed Prospects. *Population Bulletin* 45(1), June 1990.

Boyce, W., C. Schaeffer, H.R. Harrison, *et al.*
1986   Social/Cultural Factors in Pregnancy Complications Among Navajo Women. *American Journal of Epidemiology* 124:242–253.

Boyd, D.L., J.E. Maynard and L.M. Holmes
1968   Accident Mortality in Alaska. *Archives of Environmental Health* 17:101–106.

Brenner, C., K.S. Reisinger and K.D. Rogers
1973   Navajo Infant Mortality, 1970. *Public Health Reports* 89(4):353–359.

Broudy, D.W. and P.A. May
1983   Demographic and Epidemiologic Transition Among the Navajo Indians. *Social Biology* 30(1):1–16.

Brown, R.C., B.S. Gurunanjappa, R.J. Hawk and D. Bitsuie
1970   The Epidemiology of Accidents Among the Navajo Indians. *Public Health Reports* 85:881–888.

Bullough, V.L. and B. Bullough
1982   *Health Care for the Other Americans*. Chapter 5. Native Americans. Appleton-Century-Crofts, New York, NY, pp. 92–115.

Bureau of the Census
1952   *Historical Statistics of the United States: 1789–1945*. U.S. Department of Commerce. U.S. Government Printing Office, Washington, DC.

Bureau of the Census
1982   *General Population Characteristics, United States Summary* (PC80–1–B1). U.S. Department of Commerce. U.S. Government Printing Office, Washington, DC, Table 40.

Bureau of the Census
1984   *American Indian Areas and Alaska Native Villages: 1980*. (PC80–51–13). U.S. Department of Commerce. U.S. Government Printing Office, Washington, DC.

Burton, L.M.
1990   Teenage Childbearing as an Alternative Life-Course Strategy in Multigeneration Black Families. *Human Nature* 1(2):123–142.

Caldwell, J.C.
1982   *Theory of Fertility Decline*. Academic Press, New York, NY.

Carr, B. and E. Lee
1978   Navajo Tribe Mortality: A Life Table Analysis of the Leading Causes of Death. *Social Biology* 25:279–87.

Chahnazarian, A.
1988   Determinants of the Sex Ratio at Birth: Review of Recent Literature. *Social Biology* 35(3–4):214–235.

Coale, A.J.
1973   The Demographic Transition Reconsidered. *Proceedings of the International Population Conference*, Liege, Belgium, pp. 53–57.

Conte, C.
1982   Ladies, Livestock, Land and Lucre: Women's Networks
            and Social Status on the Western Navajo Reservation.
            American Indian Quarterly 6:105–124.

Coulehan, J.L., R.H. Michaels, C. Hallowell, *et al.*
1984   Epidemiology of *Haemophilus* Influenza Type B Disease
            Among Navajo Indians. *Public Health Reports* 99(4):404–
            409.

Cowen, R.
1990   Seeds of Protection. *Science News* 137:350–351.

Cowgill, D.O.
1963   Transition Theory as General Population Theory. *Social
            Forces* 41:270–274.

Davis, K.
1963   The Theory of Change and Response in Modern
            Demographic History. *Population Index* 29(4):345–366.

Dizmang, L.H., J. Watson, P.A. May and J. Bopp
1974   Adolescent Suicide at an Indian Reservation. *American
            Journal of Orthopsychiatry* 44(1):43–49.

Dobyns, H.F.
1966   Estimating Aboriginal American Population: An
            Appraisal of Techniques with a New Hemispheric
            Estimate. *Current Anthropology* 7:395–416.

Dobyns, H.F.
1976   *Native American Historical Demography: A Critical
            Bibliography*. Indiana University Press, Bloomington, IN.

Downs, J.F.
1972   *The Navajo*. Holt, Rinehart, and Winston, New York, NY.

Draper, P.
1989   African Marriage Systems: Perspectives from
            Evolutionary Ecology. *Ethnology and Sociobiology* 10:145–
            169.

Draper, P. and H. Harpending
1982   Father Absence and Reproductive Strategy: An Evolutionary Approach. *Journal of Anthropological Research* 38(3):255–273.

Driver, H.E.
1968   On the Population Nadir of Indians in the United States. *Current Anthropology* 9:330.

Eberstein, W., C.B. Nam and R.A. Hummer
1990   Infant Mortality by Cause of Death: Main and Interaction Effects. *Demography* 27(3):413–440.

Erickson, K.T.
1966   *Wayward Puritans*. John Wiley & Sons, New York, NY.

Fleshman, J.K. and D.R. Peterson
1977   The Sudden Infant Death Syndrome Among Alaska Natives. *American Journal of Epidemiology* 105(6):555–558.

Freedman, R.
1979   Theories of Fertility Decline: A Reappraisal. *Social Forces* 58:1–17.

Fricke, T.E.
1990   Darwinian Transitions? A Comment. *Population and Development Review* 16(1):107–119.

Geronimus, A.T.
1987   On Teenage Childbearing and Neonatal Mortality in the United States. *Population and Development Review* 13(2):245–279.

Goldscheider, C. and P.R. Uhlenberg
1969   Minority Group Status and Fertility. *American Journal of Sociology* 74(4):361–372.

Griffen, J.
1982   Life is Harder Here. *American Indian Quarterly* 6:90–104.

Guttentag, M. and P.F. Secord
1983   *Too Many Women? The Sex Ratio Question*. Sage Publications, Beverly Hills, CA.

Hackenberg, R.A.
1966   An Anthropological Study of the Demographic Transition: The Papago Information System. *Milbank Memorial Fund Quarterly* 44:470–493.

Hackenberg, R.A. and M.M. Gallagher
1972   The Costs of Cultural Change: Accidental Injury and Modernization Among the Papago Indians. *Human Organization* 31(2):211–226.

Hadley, J.N.
1957   Demography of the American Indian. *Annals of American Academy of Political and Social Science* 311:23–30.

Handwerker, W.P. (ed.)
1986   *Culture and Reproduction: An Anthropological Critique of Demographic Transition Theory.* Westview Press, Boulder, CO.

Hanis, C.L., R.E. Ferrell, S.A. Barton, *et al.*
1983   Diabetes Among Mexican Americans in Starr County Texas. *American Journal of Epidemiology* 118:659–672.

Harpending, H.C., P. Draper and R. Pennington
1990   Cultural Evolution, Parental Care, and Mortality. In: *Health and Disease of Populations in Transition* (G. Armelago and A. Swedland, eds.). Bergin & Garveu, South Hadley, MA.

Harris, M.
1971   *Culture, Man, and Nature.* Thomas Y. Crowell Company, New York, NY.

Hartford, R.B.
1987   The Case of the Elusive Infant Mortality Rate. In: *Perspectives on Population: An Introduction to Concepts and Issues* (S.W. Menard and E.W. Moen, eds.). Oxford University Press, New York, NY, pp. 153–155.

Hesser, J.E., B.S. Blumberg and J.S. Drew
1975   Hepatitis B Surface Antigen, Fertility and Sex Ratio: Implications for Health Planning. In: *Anthropological*

Studies of Human Fertility (B.A. Kaplan, ed.). Wayne State University Press, Detroit, MI.

Hill, C.A., Jr. and M.I. Spector
1971   Natality and Mortality of American Indians Compared with U. S. Whites and Nonwhites. *HSMHA Health Reports* 86:229–246.

Hillery, G.A., Jr. and F. Essene
1963   Navajo Population: An Analysis of the 1960 Census. *Southwest Journal of Anthropology* 19:297–313.

Hrdlicka, A.
1908   Physiological and Medical Observations Among the Indians of Southwestern United States and Northern Mexico. *Smithsonian Institution Bureau of American Ethnology*, Bulletin 34. U.S. Government Printing Office, Washington, DC.

Huber, J.
1990   Macro-Micro Links in Gender Stratification. *American Sociological Review* 55:1–10.

Indian Health Service
1984   *American Indian and Alaskan Native Life Expectancy, 1979–1981 and Life Expectancy for Selected U.S. Populations by Race, 1980.* U.S. Department of Health and Human Services, Public Health Service, Indian Health Service, Program Statistics Branch, April, 1984.

Indian Health Service
1989   *Trends in Indian Health, 1989.* U.S. Department of Health and Human Services, Public Health Service, Indian Health Service, Office of Planning, Evaluation, and Legislation, Division of Program Statistics.

Iverson, P.
1981   *The Navajo Nation.* University of New Mexico Press, Albuquerque, NM.

James, W.H.
1980   Time of Fertilization and Sex of Infants. *Lancet* 1:1124–1126.

James, W.H.
1984   Seasonality in Sex Ratio of U.S. Black Births. *Annals of Human Biology* 11(1):67–69.

James, W.H.
1984   The Sex Ratio of Black Births. *Annals of Human Biology* 11(1):39–44.

Johansson, S.R. and S.H. Preston
1978   Tribal Demography: The Hopi and Navajo Populations as Seen Through the Manuscripts from the 1900 U.S. Census. *Social Science History* 111:1–33.

Johansson, S.R.
1982   The Demographic History of the Native Peoples of North America: A Selective Bibliography. *Yearbook of Physical Anthropology* 25:133–152.

Johnson, B.M., ed.

1970   *Papers on Navajo Culture and Life*. Tsaile, AZ: Navajo Community College Press.

Johnson, J.H.
1987   U.S. Differentials in Infant Mortality: Why Do They Persist? *Family Planning Perspectives* 19(5):227–232.

Johnston, D.F.
1966   An Analysis of Sources of Information on the Population of the Navajo. *Smithsonian Institution Bureau of American Ethnology*. Bulletin 197. U.S. Government Printing Office, Washington, DC.

Kaltenbach, C.M.
1975   *Health Problems of the Navajo Area and Suggested Interventions: A Report of the AHEC*. Navajo Health Authority, Window Rock, AZ.

Kammeyer, K.C.W. and H. Ginn
1986   *An Introduction to Population*. The Dorsey Press, Chicago, IL.

Kaplan, D.W., A.E. Bauman and H.F. Krons
1984   Epidemiology of Sudden Infant Death Syndrome in
          American Indians. *Pediatrics* 74 (6):1041–1046.

Kennedy, R.E., Jr.
1973   Minority Group Status and Fertility: The Irish. *American
          Sociological Review* 38:85–96.

Kleinman, J.C. and A. Kopstein
1987   Smoking During Pregnancy, 1967–80. *American Journal
          of Public Health* 77(7):823–25.

Kleinman, J.C. and J.H. Madans
1985   The Effects of Maternal Smoking, Physical Stature, and
          Educational Attainment on the Incidence of Low Birth-
          weight. *American Journal of Epidemiology* 21(6):843–55.

Kleinman, J.C., M.B. Pierre and J.H. Madans, *et al.*
1988   The Effects of Maternal Smoking on Fetal and Infant
          Mortality. *American Journal of Epidemiology* 127(2):274–
          282.

Kluckhohn, C. and D. Leighton
1962   *The Navaho* (Revised Edition). The Natural History
          Library and Anchor Books, Doubleday and Company, Inc.,
          Garden City, NY.

Kroeber, A.L.
1939   Cultural and Natural Areas of Native North America.
          *University of California Publications in American
          Archeology and Ethnology* 38:1–242.

Kunitz, S.J.
1974a   Factors Influencing Recent Navajo and Hopi Population
          Changes. *Human Organization* 33:7–16.

Kunitz, S.J.
1974b   Navajo and Hopi Fertility, 1971–1972. *Human Biology*
          46(3):435–451.

Kunitz, S.J.
1981   Underdevelopment, Demographic Change, and Health
          Care on the Navajo Indian Reservation. *Social Science
          Medicine* 15(2):175–192.

Kunitz, S.J.
1983   *Disease Change and the Role of Medicine: The Navajo Experience*. University of California Press, Berkeley, CA.

Kunitz, S.J. and J.C. Slocumb
1975   The Use of Surgery to Avoid Childbearing among Navajo and Hopi Indians. In: *Anthropological Studies of Human Fertility*, B.A. Kaplan (ed.). Wayne State University Press, Detroit, MI.

Kunitz, S.J. and J.C. Slocumb
1976   The Changing Sex Ratio of the Navajo Tribe. *Social Biology* 23:33–44.

Lamphere, L.
1974   Strategies, Cooperation, and Conflict Among Women in Domestic Groups. In: *Woman, Culture, and Society* (M.Z. Rosaldo and L. Lamphere, eds.). Stanford University Press, Stanford, CA.

Lamphere, L.
1977   *To Run After Them: The Cultural and Social Bases of Cooperation in a Navajo Community*. University of Arizona Press, Tucson, AZ.

Lancaster, J.B.
1989   Evolutionary and Cross-Cultural Perspectives on Single Parenthood. In: *Sociobiology and the Social Sciences* (R.B. Bell, ed.). Texas Tech University Press, Lubbock, TX.

Lancaster, J.B. and C.S. Lancaster
1983   Parental Investment: The Hominid Adaptation. In: *How Humans Adapt: A Biocultural Odyssey* (D.J. Orner, ed.). Smithsonian Institution Press, Washington, DC.

Lancaster, J.B. and C.S. Lancaster
1987   The Watershed: Change in Parental-Investment and Family-Formation Strategies in the Course of Human Evolution. In: *Parenting Across the Life Span: Biosocial Dimensions* (J. Lancaster, J. Altmann, A. Rossi and L. Sherrod, eds.). Aldine de Gruyter, New York, NY, pp. 187–205.

Leighton, D. and C. Kluckhohn
1947   *Children of the People: The Navaho Individual and His Development.* Harvard University Press, Cambridge, MA.

Levy, J.E.
1965   Navajo Suicide. *Human Organization* 24:308–318.

Levy, J.E. and S.J. Kunitz
1971   Indian Reservations, Anomie, and Social Pathologies. *Southwestern Journal of Anthropology* 27(2):97–127.

Levy, J.E. and S.J. Kunitz
1974   *Indian Drinking: Navajo Practices and Anglo American Theories.* John Wiley & Sons, New York, NY.

Lujan, C., L.M. DeBruyn, P.A. May and M.E. Bird
1989   Profile of Abused and Neglected American Indian Children in the Southwest. *Child Abuse & Neglect* 13:449–461.

MacAndrew, C. and R.B. Edgerton
1969   *Drunken Comportment: A Sociological Explanation.* Aldine Publishing Company, Chicago, IL.

Manson, S.M. and N.G. Dinges (eds.)
1989   Behavioral Health Issues Among American Indians and Alaska Natives: Explorations on the Frontiers of Biobehavioral Sciences. *The Journal of the National Center*, Monograph Series, Volume I. National Center: Denver, CO.

Mauldin, W.P. and B. Berelson
1978   Conditions of Fertility Decline in Developing Countries 1965–1975. *Studies in Family Planning* 9(5):92–130.

May, P.A.
1976   *Alcohol Legalization and Native Americans: A Sociological Inquiry.* Unpublished Ph.D. Dissertation. University of Montana, Missoula, MT.

May, P.A.
1982   Substance Abuse and American Indians: Prevalence and Susceptibility. *The International Journal of Addictions* 17(7):1185–1209.

May, P.A.
1986   Alcohol and Drug Misuse Prevention Programs for
            American Indians: Needs and Opportunities. *Journal of
            Studies on Alcohol* 47(3):187–195.

May, P.A.
1987a   The Health Status of Indian Children: Problems and
            Prevention in Early Life. In: *Behavioral Health Issues
            Among American Indians and Alaska Natives:
            Explorations on the Frontiers of the Biobehavioral
            Sciences* (S.M. Manson and N.G. Dinges, eds.). American
            Indian and Alaska Native Mental Health Research.
            Monograph No. 1, pp. 244–289.

May, P.A.
1987b   Suicide and Self-Destruction Among American Indian
            Youths. *American Indian and Alaska Native Mental
            Health Research* 1(1):52–69.

May, P.A.
1989   Motor Vehicle Crashes and Alcohol Among American
            Indians and Alaska Natives. In: *The Surgeon General's
            Workshop on Drunk Driving: Background Papers.* Office of
            the Surgeon General, U.S. Public Health Service, U.S.
            Department of Health and Human Services, Washington,
            DC.

May, P.A. and L.H. Dizmang
1974   Suicide and the American Indian. *Psychiatric Annals*
            4(9):22–28.

May, P.A., K.J. Hymbaugh, J.M. Aase and J.M. Samet
1983   Epidemiology of Fetal Alcohol Syndrome Among American
            Indians of the Southwest. *Social Biology* 30(4):374–387.

May, P.A. and M.B. Smith
1988   Some Navajo Indian Opinions About Alcohol Abuse and
            Prohibition: A Survey and Recommendations for Policy.
            Journal of Studies on Alcohol 49(4):324–334.

McCormick, M.C.
1985   The Contribution of Low Birth Weight to Infant Mortality and Childhood Mortality. *New England Journal of Medicine* 312:82–90.

McKinlay, J.B.
1974   A Case for Refocussing Upstream: The Political Economy of Illness. In: *The Sociology of Health and Illness* (C. Conrad and R. Kern, eds., 1981). St. Martin's Press, New York, NY.

McPherson, R.S.
1988   *The Northern Navajo Frontier 1860–1900: Expansion Through Adversity*. University of New Mexico Press, Albuquerque, NM.

Metcalf, A.
1982   Navajo Women in the City: Lessons from a Quarter-Century of Relocation. *American Indian Quarterly* 6:71–89.

Mohatt, G.
1972   The Sacred Water: The Quest for Personal Power Through Drinking Among Teton Sioux. In: *The Drinking Man* (D.C. McClelland, W.N. Davis, R. Kalin and E. Wanner, eds.). The Free Press, New York, NY, pp. 261–275.

Mooney, J.
1928   The Aboriginal Population of America North of Mexico. In: *Smithsonian Miscellaneous Collections* (J.R. Swanton, ed.). Washington, DC, 80:1–40.

Morgan, K.
1973   Historical Demography of a Navajo Community. *Methods and Theories of Anthropological Genetics* (M.H. Crawford and P.L. Workman, eds.). University of New Mexico Press, Albuquerque, NM, pp. 263–314.

Nam, C.B. and S.G. Philliber
1984   *Population: A Basic Orientation* (Second Edition). Prentice-Hall, Inc., Englewood Cliffs, NJ.

National Academy of Sciences
1981   Committee on Population and Demography. Report Number 4. National Academy Press, Washington, DC.

National Academy of Sciences
1985   *Injury in America: A Continuing Public Health Problem.* National Academy Press, Washington, DC.

National Center for Health Statistics
1988   *Vital Statistics of the United States, 1985.* Volumes 1 and 2, Natality and Mortality, Part A. DHHS Pub. Nos. (PHS)88–1101 and 88–1113. Public Health Service. U.S. Government Printing Office, Washington, DC.

National Center for Health Statistics
1989   *Health, United States, 1988.* DHHS Pub. No. (PHS) 89–1232. Public Health Service. U.S. Government Printing Office, Washington, DC.

Navajo Nation
1988   *Navajo Nation FAX 88.* Technical Support Department, Division of Community Development, Navajo Nation, Window Rock, AZ.

Neel, J.V.
1962   Diabetes Mellitus: a "Thrifty" Genotype Rendered Detrimental by "Progress." *American Journal of Human Genetics* 14:353–362.

New Mexico Health & Environment Department
1990   *New Mexico Monthly Vital Statistics Report.* Public Health Division, Vital Records and Statistics, Santa Fe, NM, July, 1990.

New Mexico Department of Health
1992   *1990 New Mexico Tribe Specific Vital Statistics.* Office of Vital Records and Health Statistics, Santa Fe, NM, February, 1992.

Niswander, J.D., M.V. Barrow and S.J. Bingle
1975   Congenital Malformations in the American Indian. *Social Biology* 22 (3):203–215.

Niswander, J.D. and L. Woodville
1973   Prenatal Care, Birth Weight, Major Malformation and Newborn Death in American Indians. *HSMHA Health Reports* 88(8):697–701.

Omran, A.R.
1971   The Epidemiologic Transition: A Theory of the Epidemiology of Population Change. *Milbank Memorial Fund Quarterly* 49(4):509–538.

Omran, A.
1980   Epidemiologic Transition in the United States: The Health Factor in Population Change. *Population Bulletin* 32(2):1–44. (Population Reference Bureau, Inc., Washington, DC, May 1980 updated reprint.)

Omran, A. and B. Loughlin
1972   Epidemiologic Studies of Accidents Among Navajo Indians. *Journal of the Egyptian Medical Association* 55(1):1–22.

Passel, J.S.
1976   Provisional Evaluation of the 1970 Census Count of American Indians. *Demography* 13:397–409.

Passel, J.S. and P.A. Berman
1986   Quality of 1980 Census Data for American Indians. *Social Biology* 33:163–182.

Pennington, R. and H. Harpending
1988   Fitness and Fertility Among Kalahari !Kung. American *Journal of Physical Anthropology* 77:303–319.

Piche, V.
1973   Estimates of Vital Rates for the Canadian Indians 1960–1970. *Demography* 10:367–382.

Polgar, S.
1962   Health and Human Behavior: Areas of Interest Common to the Social and Medical Sciences. *Current Anthropology* 3(2):159–198.

Red Horse, J.G.
1980   Family Structure and Value Orientation in American
        Indians. *Social Casework* 61:462–471.

Ritchey, P.N.
1975   The Effect of Minority Group Status on Fertility: A
        Reexamination of Concepts. *Population Studies*
        29(July):249–257.

Roberts, R.E. and E.S. Lee
1974   Minority Group Status and Fertility Revisited. *American
        Journal of Sociology* 80(2):503–523.

Rogers, R.G.
1989   Ethnic and Birth Weight Differences in Cause-Specific
        Infant Mortality. *Demography* 26(2):335–343.

Rogers, R.G. and R. Hackenberg
1987   Extending Epidemiologic Transition Theory: A New
        Stage. *Social Biology* 34:234–243.

Romanuik, A.
1981   Increase in Natural Fertility During the Early Stages of
        Modernization: Canadian Indians Case Study.
        Demography 18:157–180.

Rosen, L.S. and K. Gorwitz
1980   New Attention to American Indians. *American
        Demographics* 2:18–25.

Samet, J.M., C.R. Key, D.M. Kutvirt and C.L. Wiggins
1980   Respiratory Disease Mortality in New Mexico's American
        Indians and Hispanics. *American Journal of Public
        Health* 70:492–497.

Samet, J.M., C.R. Key, W.C. Hunt and J.S. Goodwin
1987   Survival of American Indian and Hispanic Cancer
        Patients in New Mexico and Arizona, 1969–82. *Journal of
        the National Cancer Institute* 70:457–463.

Samet, J.M., D.B. Coultas, C.A. Howard, *et al.*
1988   Diabetes, Gallbladder Disease, Obesity, and Hypertension
        Among Hispanics in New Mexico. *American Journal of
        Epidemiology* 128:1302–1311.

Scheper-Hughes, N.
1985   Culture, Scarcity, and Maternal Thinking: Mother Love
          and Child Death in Northeast Brazil. In: *Child Survival*
          (N. Scheper-Hughes, ed.). American Anthropological
          Association, pp. 187–208.

Sewell, C.M., T.M. Becker, C.L. Wiggins, *et al.*
1989   Injury Mortality in New Mexico's American Indians,
          Hispanics, and non-Hispanic Whites, 1958 to 1982.
          Western Journal of Medicine 150:708–713.

Shepardson, M.
1982   The Status of Navajo Women. *American Indian Quarterly*
          6:149–169.

Shore, J.H.
1975   American Indian Suicide—Fact and Fantasy. *Psychiatry*
          38:86–91.

Siegel, B.J., A.R. Beals and S.A. Tyler
1972   Demographic Studies in Anthropology. *American Review
          of Anthropology* 1:151–178.

Slocumb, J. and S. Kunitz
1977   Factors Affecting Maternal Mortality and Morbidity
          Among American Indians. *Public Health Reports*
          92(4):349–356.

Sly, D.F.
1970   Minority Group Status and Fertility: An Extension of
          Goldscheider and Uhlenberg. *American Journal of
          Sociology* 76:443–459.

Snipp, C.M.
1989   *American Indians: The First of This Land*. Russell Sage
          Foundation, New York, NY.

Sorkin, A.L.
1969   Some Aspects of American Indian Migration. *Social
          Forces* 48:243–250.

Sorkin, A.L.
1976   The Economic and Social Status of the American Indian
          1940–1970. *Journal of Negro Education* 45:432–447.

Sowell, T.
1981	*Ethnic America: A History*. Basic Books, New York, NY.

Spencer, R.F. and J.D. Jennings, *et al.*
1977	*The Native Americans* (Second Edition). Harper & Row, New York, NY.

Stack, C.B.
1974	*All Our Kin: Strategies for Survival in a Black Community*. Harper and Row, New York, NY.

Stanley, S. and R.K. Thomas
1978	Current Demographic and Social Trends Among North American Indians. *Annals of American Academy of Political and Social Sciences* 436:111–120.

Stark, O.
1981	The Asset Demand for Children During Agricultural Modernization. *Population and Development Review* 7:671–675.

Stephen, E.H.
1987	Patterns of American Indian Fertility: Theoretical Approaches to Explain Extant High Fertility in an Indigenous Population. Presented at the Annual Meeting of the Population Association of America, Chicago, IL, April 29–May 2, 1987.

Stewart, O.C. and D.F. Aberle
1984	*Peyotism in the West*. Anthropological Paper Number 108. University of Utah Press, Salt Lake City, UT.

Stewart, T., P. May and A. Muneta
1980	A Navajo Health Consumer Survey. *Medical Care* 18(12): 1183–1195.

Stucki, L.R.
1971	The Case Against Population Control: The Probable Creation of the First American Indian State. *Human Organization* 30:393–399.

Teitelbaum, M.S.
1975	Relevance of Demographic Transition for Developing Countries. *Science* 188(4187):420–425.

Temkin-Greener, H., S.J. Kunitz, D. Broudy and M. Haffner
1981   Surgical Fertility Regulation Among Women on the Navajo Reservation, 1972–1978. *American Journal of Public Health* 71:403–407.

Terrell, J.U.
1970   *The Navajos.* Weybright and Talley, New York, NY.

Thornton, R.
1987   *American Indian Holocaust and Survival: A Population History Since 1492.* University of Oklahoma Press, Norman, OK.

Thornton, R. and J. Marsh-Thorton
1981   Estimating Prehistoric American Indian Population Size for United States Area: Implications of the Nineteenth Century Population Decline and Nadir. *American Journal of Physical Anthropology* 55:47–53.

Torrez, D.J.
1990   *Sudden Infant Death Syndrome in New Mexico (1975–1985).* Unpublished Dissertation. University of New Mexico, Albuquerque, NM.

Tsai, S.P., E.S. Lee and R.J. Hardy
1978   The Effect of a Reduction in Leading Causes of Death: Potential Gains in Life Expectancy. *American Journal of Public Health* 68:966–971.

Turke, P.W.
1989   Evolution and the Demand for Children. *Population and Development Review* 15(1):61–90.

Ubelaker, D.H.
1976   Prehistoric New World Population Size: Historical Review and Current Appraisal of North American Estimates. *American Journal of Physical Anthropology* 45:661–666.

Ubelaker, D.H.
1988   North American Indian Population Size, AD 1500 to 1985. *American Journal of Physical Anthropology* 77(3):289–294.

Underhill, R.M.
1956   *The Navajos.* University of Oklahoma Press, Norman, OK.

Vanlandingham, M.J., J.W. Buehler, C.J.R. Hogue and L.T. Strauss
1988   Birthweight-specific Infant Mortality for Native
          Americans Compared with Whites, Six States, 1980.
          American Journal of Public Health 78(5):499–503.

Van Winkle, N.W. and P.A. May
1986   Native American Suicide in New Mexico 1957–1979: A
          Comparative Study. *Human Organization* 45(4):296–309.

Waddell, J.O. and M.W. Everett (eds.)
1980   *Drinking Behavior Among Southwestern Indians: An
          Anthropological Perspective.* University of Arizona Press,
          Tucson, AZ.

Ward, J.A. and J. Fox
1977   A Suicide Epidemic on an Indian Reserve. *Canadian
          Psychiatric Association Journal* 22:423–426.

Warren, C.W., H.I. Goldberg, L. Oge, D. Pepion, *et al.*
1990   Assessing the Reproductive Behavior of On- and Off-
          Reservation American Indian Females: Characteristics of
          Two Groups in Montana. *Social Biology* 37(1–2):69–83.

Wasser, S.K.
1990   Infertility, Abortion, and Biotechnology. *Human Nature*
          1(1):3–24.

Wasser, S.K. and D.Y. Isenberg
1986   Reproductive Failure among Women: Pathology or
          Adaptation? *Journal of Psychosomatic Obstetrics and
          Gynaecology* 5:153–175.

Waxweiller, R.J. and R.J. Roscoe
1981   Secondary Sex Ratio of First-born Offspring of U.S.
          Uranium Miners. In: *Birth Defects in the Four Corners
          Area* (W.H. Wiese, ed.). Transcript of a meeting.
          University of New Mexico School of Medicine,
          Albuquerque, NM.

Weeks, J.R.
1989   *Population: An Introduction to Concepts and Issues* (Fourth Edition). Wadsworth Publishing Company, Belmont, CA.

West, K.M.
1974   Diabetes in American Indians and Other Native Populations of the New World. *Diabetes* 23:841–847.

White, R. and D. Cornely
1981   Navajo Child Abuse and Neglect Study. *Child Abuse and Neglect* 5:9–17.

Woods, O.
1947   Health Among the Navajo Indians. *Journal of the American Medical Association* 135:981–83.

Wright, A.
1982   An Ethnography of the Navajo Reproductive Cycle. *American Indian Quarterly* 6:52–70.

Yazzie, E. (ed.)
1971   *Navajo History* (Volume 1). Navajo Community College Press, Many Farms, AZ.

Yinger, J.M. and G.E. Simpson
1978   The Integration of Americans of Indian Descent. *Annals of American Academy of Political and Social Sciences* 436:137–151.